God Said, "I AM"

A Look at the Divinity of Christ

By
Terry A. Morris

Copyright © 2016 by Terry A. Morris

God said, "I AM"
A Look at the Divinity of Christ
by Terry A. Morris

Printed in the United States of America.

Edited by Xulon Press.

ISBN 9781498487719

All rights reserved solely by the author. The author guarantees all contents are original and do not infringe upon the legal rights of any other person or work. No part of this book may be reproduced in any form without the permission of the author. The views expressed in this book are not necessarily those of the publisher.

Scripture quotations taken from the New International Version (NIV). Copyright © 1973, 1978, 1984, 2011 by Biblica, Inc.™. Used by permission. All rights reserved.

www.xulonpress.com

DEDICATION

Dedicated to my lovely wife, Sandy, who was a constant encourager in spite of having to share me for the years it took to write this book. She also acted as editor and sounding board and provided valuable feedback. I also dedicate this book to my good friend and brother in Christ, Rev. Dwight Shirey, for all his prayers, emotional support, encouragement, and editing skills. "Papa D," as he was known by all who loved him, had a significant role in shaping my future. The times we met for prayer and Bible study were among some of my greatest memories. In 2012, Papa D passed from this life to his eternal reward, but his absence is still felt.

CONTENTS

INTRODUCTION..xv
CHAPTER 1: A MOUNTAIN ON FIRE 19
CHAPTER 2: JESUS IDENTIFIES HIMSELF................... 24
CHAPTER 3: DIALOGUE WITH THE JEWS................. 33
CHAPTER 4: I AM THE BREAD OF LIFE 45
CHAPTER 5: I AM THE LIGHT OF THE WORLD 52
CHAPTER 6: I AM THE DOOR 59
CHAPTER 7: I AM THE GOOD SHEPHERD................. 64
CHAPTER 8: I AM THE RESURRECTION AND
    THE LIFE 72
CHAPTER 9: I AM THE WAY, THE TRUTH, AND
    THE LIFE 77
CHAPTER 10: I AM THE TRUE VINE....................... 84

CONCLUSION 89
ENDNOTES 95
BIBLIOGRAPHY 101

FOREWORD

*I*n reading John 14:17–18, it is clear that we Christ followers are to be the presence of Jesus in the world. In John 17:20–23, we see this again and expanded. The clear implication is that we are to be the real and living presence of Jesus in the world. The importance in reading this book is to see more clearly Jesus' descriptions of Himself, His person, His call, and His divinity. As we understand the person of Jesus more clearly, then we can be His person in this world, sharing truth, bringing light, leading to the door to the eternal, and bringing life to a world with so much death. In addition, we can be so much more aware of all that is ours because we walk with Jesus. Imagine a person in a wilderness with no food or drink. They have only on their back a pack that they were told would bring good things to them as they walk across the wilderness to a promised land. In the middle of the wilderness, they give up, sit down, and die of thirst. Sometime later their body is found with the backpack lying nearby. When the backpack is opened, water and food are found. The wanderer had never opened it to see its lifesaving contents. So it is with us. So often we do not know the richness of the person of Jesus and what He has given us to walk through this wilderness of life. As you read this book and absorb the reality of the person of Jesus, drink freely and eat to your fill, for this will give you the sustenance to make it through this wilderness of life.

—Harold Rhoades, PhD, LP,
adjunct professor at Emmanuel College

PREFACE

*I*t has been said that a picture is worth a thousand words. You could try to explain to a young child what a duckbill platypus looks like, but it is doubtful they would grasp as clear an understanding as simply showing them a picture. When we combine the concept of pictures with a verbal description, we are able to create what is known as "word pictures." Poets have used this form of speech for centuries.

I became fascinated with word pictures with my first Old Testament survey class, whether it was God's promise to Moses to lead the children of Israel to a land flowing with milk and honey (Ex. 3:8), or a young shepherd boy named David reflecting on God as his own shepherd (Psalm 23). A vivid picture was imprinted on the mind that words alone could not produce.

Nowhere is this more evident than in the teachings of Jesus. With the skill of a great artist, Jesus paints one masterpiece after another on the canvases of our hearts and minds. This is what drew me to the "I AM" sayings of Jesus. When it came time to choose a topic for my master's thesis, I looked no further than the gospel of John. However, even after I received a passing grade, the images portrayed in Jesus' self-description captivated my mind. This book is the result of my own fascination with Jesus' word pictures.

It is my prayer that you will be equally blessed as you walk through John's picture gallery of Jesus. May you look deeply into each portrait as these images come alive in your heart. What do they say about Jesus, and what does that mean for you today?

—Terry A. Morris

ACKNOWLEDGMENTS

Special thanks to Jake Terlecki for his spectacular artwork, to my daughter Virginia Brice, my daughters-in-law Bev Morris and Deanna Ingerham Rees for their editing skills, and Mara East for her proofreading. These ladies have been a special blessing to me. Most of all I praise God for His guiding hand on my life and direction in writing this book.

INTRODUCTION

The divinity of the Lord Jesus Christ is the core doctrine of the Christian church. On this central doctrine hinge all the other doctrines of our faith. All that we believe, regardless of denomination, is based on who Jesus really is. There is no room here for halfhearted faith. Either Jesus is who He says He is, or He is a liar. Our acceptance of Him as the Christ is either "Yes, He is" or "No, He isn't." There is no middle ground here, and each person must make that determination based on the information provided in God's Word. This is the basis for this book.

I have always been fascinated by the images that Jesus paints in the Gospels. He chose each image for a specific purpose and to communicate a specific truth. I believe that through these many word paintings, Jesus identifies who He is and how that truth relates to each one of us. However, accepting that truth is our part, and there have been many who have refused to do that.

Even before the birth of the church, the divine nature of Jesus was under attack. As He walked through the Palestine countryside with His disciples, there were those who consistently challenged His authority. John states in his gospel, "He came to that which was his own, but his own did not receive him" (John 1:11). Sitting in a synagogue in His hometown of

Nazareth, He opened the Scriptures to the prophet Isaiah and read, "The Spirit of the Lord is on me because he has anointed me to preach good news to the poor. He has sent me to proclaim freedom for the prisoners and recovery of sight for the blind, to release the oppressed, to proclaim the year of the Lord's favor" (Luke 4:18–19). Then, to the shock of all those present, He said, "Today this Scripture is fulfilled in your hearing." Their response says it all: "Isn't this Joseph's son?" All they could see was flesh and blood.

With the birth of the church, the attacks only intensified. Acknowledging that Jesus was an extraordinary man who performed many good and noble deeds, many denied He was God. As early as AD 325, the church leaders were forced to deal with false doctrines concerning the nature of Jesus Christ. Many heresies had been circulating through the churches. The Nicene Council was convened to deal with the Arian controversy. Arius believed that Jesus was an incarnation of a previously existent being named "The Logos" and was of a different nature from God or man.[1]

The council, of course, rejected this view, yet it resurfaced at different times through church history under different names. In fact, most of the heresies that have surfaced through history concerning the divinity of Jesus Christ are simply reoccurrences of like doctrines refashioned in modern terminology—new people using old arguments with a new twist.

The Ebionites were another early group that denied Jesus' nature. This was actually a Jewish sect who believed in the messiahship of Christ but rejected the idea that He was divine. They believed that Jesus was chosen to be the Messiah at His baptism and was at that time given an unmeasured fullness of the Holy Spirit.[2] Jesus as a mere man inspired by God is seen in the doctrine of Apollinarius (AD 390). He believed that if Christ possessed a rational soul, He could not truly be God.[3] This view was reborn in the 1500s by Laelius and Faustus Socinus, who stated that Jesus was a "divinized man," a man who had been given "extraordinary revelations."[4] Such beliefs are held today by many different forms of liberal theologies and by the New Age philosophies. These false doctrines have been rebuffed by church leaders of every era. Today the attacks appear more vicious than ever, taking on the disguise of righteousness. There are many "religious" leaders who call on the Christian church to unite with those who worship God in their own way and not to be so exclusive. We are challenged to embrace those of other beliefs and announce ourselves as brothers. We are asked to put away our differences and focus on areas of likeness, but to do these things, we must betray the one who has provided us with hope. We must deny the one thing that divides us, the divinity of the Lord Jesus Christ.

While I believe there are several proofs of Christ's divinity and many good resources that describe these proofs in detail, the scope of this book is to focus on the words of Jesus Christ in His portrayal of Himself. I believe that in His use of the term "I am," He boldly and clearly announces to those who will hear that He is the Son of God, the Savior of the world. This is seen in both His terminology and in the analogies He uses to identify Himself. I will review each of the uses of "I am," beginning in Exodus, where God first revealed Himself to Moses, and follow Jesus' use of the term as recorded by the apostle John. Through the use of this term, we are able to see a portrait of Jesus, painted by His own words, which declares His true identity as the Son of the living God.

We first turn to a remote area in the land of Midian, where a shepherd for the priest of Midian was tending his flocks. Although his day probably started like any other day, this day would forever change not only the life of this shepherd, but the direction of a whole nation.

Chapter 1

A MOUNTAIN ON FIRE

The life of a shepherd was not only difficult, but also lonely. Most of the days and many evenings were spent alone with the sheep. There was certainly plenty of time for thought. As one shepherd led his sheep to the western side of the desert, one can only guess what was on his mind, but perhaps his thoughts were far off in another land. This man was not just any shepherd; he had been raised in a palace. He may have been reminiscing about the family he had left behind and the safety of his people. Having been born of Hebrew parents, he had been placed in a basket and set adrift in the Nile River.

Because of the rapidly increasing numbers of the Hebrew people, Pharaoh was concerned that they would rebel against Egypt, and then Egypt would become their slaves (Ex. 1:8). He gave an order to all the people that every male child was to be killed (1:15). One woman defied the order and hid her son for three months before putting him in a basket and praying that an Egyptian mother would have pity on him. Pulled from the Nile by Pharaoh's own daughter, this baby was given the name Moses. He was raised in the safety of Pharaoh's palace. I love the irony here. Pharaoh sought to kill all of the Hebrew male infants because he feared them, but God arranged to have Moses, the one who would lead the Hebrews out of Egypt, to be raised within Pharaoh's own household. Isn't that just like God?

When Moses actually learned his true identity, we are not told, but what we are told is he witnessed the suffering of the Hebrews under their Egyptian masters. Attempting to save a fellow Hebrew, he killed an Egyptian who was beating him (Ex. 2:12). Fearing Pharaoh's wrath, he fled to the desert of Midian, where his heroic efforts in protecting the daughters of a Midianite priest earned him not only a job, but also a wife.

It was while leading the sheep to find new pastures that he found himself near Mount Horeb, the name for a mountain range of which Mount Sinai was a part. It was here that Moses' life was about to take another dramatic change. What a contrast he had already seen from the palace of Pharaoh to wandering in a desert. Alexander Maclaren reminds us, "God tests His weapons before He uses them."[1] As Moses passed by the sheep, as he had done many times before, a strange light caught his eye. As he moved to get a closer look, he saw a bush that "burned with fire, but the bush was not consumed" (Ex. 3:2 KJV). Such bushes were abundant in that area, but to observe one aglow yet not have it consumed was enough to gain Moses' attention and to hold it. Because of the nature of the dry acacias, even a small fire would have been enough to pass through them like a flash.[2] Yet this was no ordinary fire. Exodus 3:2 states, "There the angel of the LORD appeared to him in flames of fire from within a bush."

God's use of fire to reveal Himself is seen throughout Scripture. He placed cherubim with a "flaming sword" at the entrance to the Garden of Eden to block any return by Adam and Eve (Gen. 3:24). In Genesis 15:17, God was revealed to Abraham as "a smoking firepot with a blazing torch." During the exodus from Egypt, God went before the children of Israel as a pillar of cloud by day and "a pillar of fire by night" (Ex. 13:21). Isaiah's description found in Isaiah 10:17 also reveals God in the likeness of fire: "And the light of Israel will become a fire, and their Holy One a flame."

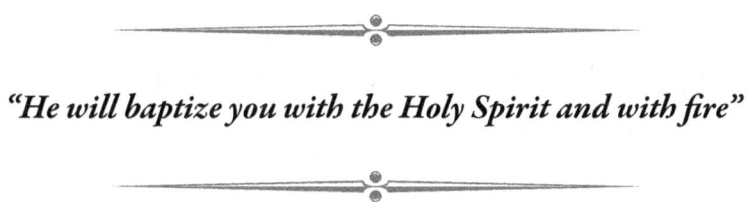

"He will baptize you with the Holy Spirit and with fire"

This image continues into the New Testament with John the Baptist speaking of Jesus, saying, "He will baptize you with the Holy Spirit, and with fire" (Matt. 3:11). We see this fulfilled at Pentecost when the disciples were gathered in the upper room and were filled with the Holy Spirit. Acts 2 records the event, and in verse 3 we read, "They saw what seemed to be tongues of fire that separated and came to rest on each of them." The Hebrew writer tells us, "For our God is a consuming fire" (Heb. 12:29). For God's purposes here, however, the bush was not consumed; it was steady and undying, and Moses was captivated by it.

God first identified Himself by saying, "I am the God of your father, the God of Abraham, the God of Isaac, and the God of Jacob" (Ex. 3:6). God acknowledged the suffering of the Hebrews and told Moses He had a plan and that this plan involved him. It was upon further discussion that Moses asked God, "Suppose I go to the Israelites and say to them, 'The God of your fathers has sent me to you,' and they ask me, 'What is his name?' Then what shall I tell them?" (v. 13). Perhaps he remembered the last response he had received when he tried to help his fellow Hebrews. Coming across two Hebrews who were fighting, he asked them why they were fighting against each other, to which one responded, "Who made you ruler and judge over us?" (Ex. 2:13–14). Now God was asking him to go to the elders of Israel and tell them God had sent him to free them, and on top of that, he was going to lead them to a land that flowed with milk and honey (v. 17). It was in the answer to this question that God first revealed this form of His name. "God said to Moses, 'I AM WHO I AM: This is what you are to say to the Israelites: "I AM has sent me to you"'" (Ex. 3:14).

"I AM WHO I AM."

Three times in this passage God referred to His name as "I AM." Here the name I AM is connected to the unspeakable name of God, YHWH. I AM does not mean Yahweh, but it is a derivative of the verb *to be*, which is where the name Yahweh comes from.³ He is the ever- present one. While man would have to say, "I am that which I have become," God says, "I AM WHO I AM."⁴ He is self-dependent, unlimited, unchangeable, and absolute. He is I AM at every point of history. Adam was, and Abraham was, and Moses was, but God is. This says so much about the nature of God. As man, we live within the confinements of time. We are born into a period of time, and we are given a life span that is divided into years, months, weeks, days, minutes, and seconds. Our whole scale of understanding is based on the concept of time. It is accurate to speak of a time when we did not exist, such as, "The Civil War was fought *before* I was born." We can even speak of a time in the future when we will still be; for example, "When I enter heaven, I *will be* with all those who have gone on before." However, it is never appropriate to refer to God as "was" or "will be," for

God always "is." Through this, He speaks of His self-existence, His mystery, and His majesty. His unapproachableness is seen in His words to Moses as he walked toward the burning bush and God said, "Do not come any closer. Take off your sandals, for the place where you are standing is holy ground" (Ex. 3:5). God places the fullest expression of His eternal being in these two words: I AM.

Although there has been some debate over the exact interpretation of the Hebrew word *ehyeh*, which is translated "I AM" in most Bible translations, there is no debate over the fact it is translated *ego eimi* in the Septuagint, the Greek translation of the Hebrew Scriptures.[5] *Ego eimi* in the Greek means "I am," and though this has a common use in Scripture, such as in Exodus 3:4 where Moses states, "Here I am," it is also used in several places through the Old Testament as a word of divine self-revelation: "I am your salvation" (Ps. 35:3); "I am merciful" (Jer. 3:12); "I, even I, am he who blots out your transgressions" (Isa. 43:25, notice the use of repetition for emphasis). The "I am" coupled with a predicate nominative makes a specific identification about the character of God.

The apostle John carried over this use into the New Testament and made specific claims about the nature of Jesus Christ. Using the Old Testament use of I AM as a foundation, we will look at John's use of "I am" with and without a predicate. It is to John's gospel that we next turn our attention.

Chapter 2

JESUS IDENTIFIES HIMSELF

"I am" coupled with a predicate nominative is one of the most important characteristics of John's gospel.[1] Whereas it occurs in the Synoptic Gospels only fourteen times combined, John uses it thirty-eight times.[2] John also uses *ego eimi* (I am) without the predicate. Philip Harner suggests two explanations: "The first solution proposes that some noun or pronoun should be understood from the context as a predicate for the phrase 'I am.'"[3] The example he gives is found in John 9:9. Jesus healed a man born blind, which raised a large debate whether this was really the same man. Some said he was the same man; others said he was like him, but a different man. The man once blind set the record straight when he said, "I am *he*." The *ego eimi* is used without the predicate, which means the "he" is not really present in the Greek. However, as Harner points out, the predicate is implied within the context that centers on the discussion, "Is it he?" Thus the comment "I am" assumes what is already known "I am [he, the one you speak of, the man]."[4]

The second way of interpreting the predicate-less *ego eimi* is in an absolute sense. Harner regards it as a "distinct, self-contained expression that is complete and meaningful in itself."[5] Harner is not alone in his view; C. H.

Dodd[6] and C. K. Barrett[7] both believe this is the correct use of *ego eimi* as used by Jesus. They refer to this use as a "theophanic formula," regarding it as representative of the divine name or presence. Therefore, through Jesus' use of the I AM phrase, He not only announced His divine nature, but also drew a direct link to His presence in the burning bush.

Before looking at the specific passages in John, it is important to note that a predicate noun in the Greek usually lacks the direct article. When it is used, it indicates that the predicate is identical with the subject rather than a general class of which the subject is a part. "Whenever the article occurs the object is certainly definite," writes Dana and Mantley.[8] By using the direct article in many of his *ego eimi* expressions, I believe that John was expressing his belief in Jesus not only as the one who defined the object, but as the one in which the object was but a shadow. For example, in John 14:6, Jesus said, "I am the way, the truth, and the life." By using the direct article, Jesus proclaimed that He is *the* way, as opposed to *a* way. We will look at each of these word pictures that Jesus created in later chapters. Before looking at these, however, there are two other ways that Jesus used the phrase "I am." First, it is used as a statement of identification (John 4:26; 6:20; 18:5), and second, in an absolute sense without the use of any predicate (John 8:24, 28, 58; 13:19). Each of these will be discussed at length, beginning with the common use of "I am" as a form of identification.

Encounter at a Well

In chapter 4 of John's gospel, we read about Jesus leaving Judea for Galilee. Verse 4 tells us, "Now he had to go through Samaria." This appears strange at first, since the Jews had no dealings with the Samaritans. Going through Samaria was the shortest route from Jerusalem to Galilee, but many Jews refused to travel that way simply because it took them through Samaria. Most scholars believe the Samaritans were a mixed race brought about by the captivity and exile of the northern kingdom. The king of Assyria deported many of the leaders from Israel, including religious leaders, and replaced them with people from foreign nations (2 Kings 17:6, 24–26). From that time on, the inhabitants of the northern kingdom had no prophetic voice, and they refused to acknowledge Jerusalem as a place of worship. The Samaritans became a fringe segment of the Jewish world. They accepted only the five books of Moses and rejected the remainder of the Old Testament. The Samaritans also had hostile feelings toward the Jews. During the time of the rebuilding of the temple in Jerusalem, the Samaritans offered their help, only to be rejected because they were not pure Jews (Ezra 4:2). After their assistance was rejected, the Samaritans opposed the rebuilding of the temple (Ezra 4:3–5; Neh. 4:1–2).

We are told later in verse 8 that the disciples had left Jesus there at Jacob's well while they went into town to buy food. The well of Jacob lay at the foot of Mount Gerizim, the center of Samaritan worship. As Jesus sat by the well, a Samaritan woman approached the well, and Jesus began a conversation with her. It did not take long before their conversation became religious in nature. He first drew her attention to the purpose of the well: "Will you give me a drink?" (v. 7). It was here that travelers would quench their thirst before moving on. The well also supplied water for the villagers of Sychar that was necessary for their livelihood. When the woman responded with surprise that a Jew would even speak to her, a Samaritan, Jesus changed the direction of the conversation from the water that the well could supply to the water that He could supply. The woman, whose name we are never given, continued to focus on the physical realm by pointing out to Jesus that He had nothing to draw water with. How could he give her this "living water"? Contrasting the difference between the water she was used to and the water that He could supply, Jesus said, "Everyone who drinks this water will be thirsty again, but whoever drinks the water I give him will never thirst. Indeed, the water I give him will become in him a spring of water welling up to eternal life" (vv. 13–14).

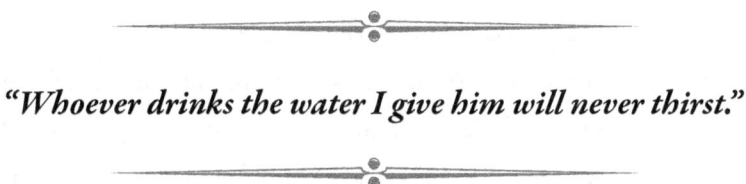

"Whoever drinks the water I give him will never thirst."

Responding to Jesus' invitation with excitement, the woman was instructed to go call her husband. This was, perhaps, an embarrassing topic for the woman. Some have speculated this was the reason she was at the well during that time of day instead of when the other village women would go for water. The "sixth hour" (v. 6) would have been about noon. It was uncommon for a woman to go to the well for water at that time, and to go alone was also dangerous. Perhaps it was her way of not having to deal with the comments from the other women. What happened next is best heard from the woman's lips herself: "I have no husband" (v. 17). Jesus at no point condemned the woman or condoned her actions, but instead acknowledged her truthfulness: "You are right when you say you have no husband. The fact is, you have had five husbands, and the man you now have is not your husband. What you have said is quite true" (v. 17). Later in the village, she would tell those who would hear her, "Come, see a man who told me everything I ever did" (v. 29).

The woman was the first to introduce the topic of the Messiah. As a Samaritan, she believed in the coming of a messiah. He was to be a teacher and a lawgiver after the tradition of Moses. She stated that when Messiah arrived, He would teach them all they needed to know (v. 25). Jesus' response became the first of the "I am" expressions used as a simple form of identification. "I who speak to you am he" (v. 26). This was also the first self-disclosure of His true identity. The statement *ego eimi* (translated "am he" in the NIV) is used as a definite messianic figure. The "he" used here is emphatic, making a reference back to "Messiah." Used in this fashion, it refers to all that the Messiah is.[9] The statement of identification that Jesus made here is very close to the one made in Isaiah 52:6. As God had predicted the captivity of His people, so He promised their return and said, "Therefore, they shall know in that day that I am he that doth speak: behold, it is I" (KJV). Certainly the woman was convinced, for in her statement to the villagers (v. 25), she also added, "Could this be the Christ?" The woman was not the only one to believe that Jesus was the Messiah, for as the villagers went out to see for themselves how accurate the woman's report was, they invited Jesus to stay with them awhile longer (v. 40). Jesus complied to their request and spent two days with the Samaritans, the results of which are seen in vs. 41, "And because of his words many more became believers." What they believed is revealed in verse 42, where speaking to the woman, they said, "We no longer believe just because of what you said; now we have heard for ourselves, and we know that this man is the Savior of the world." With Jesus' first "I AM" statement, He identified Himself as the Messiah, and there emerged the first recorded revival in the New Testament.

A Stormy Sea

Our next "I AM" statement takes us to a stormy Sea of Galilee (6:15–21). Matthew records that after Jesus had fed the multitudes, He dismissed the people and instructed the disciples to take a boat to the other side of the lake (Matt. 14:23). Jesus then went up into the mountain to pray by Himself (John 6:15). As Jesus prayed, the light faded into darkness, and the disciples struggled against a sea that was no longer calm. The Sea of Galilee is not a large body of water, and because it is located close to the mountains, it is not unusual for severe wind squalls to develop quickly.[10] Just such a squall was causing the disciples enormous effort in their attempt to get to the other side. Mark 6:48 records that they were "straining at the oars." The Greek word used here literally means "torture," "to be distressed."[11] The disciples were rowing so hard against the wind and waves that it was "torture." John records that they rowed only about three to three and half miles (v. 19), or about halfway across. Mark tells us that Jesus saw them struggling against the waves. According to Mark, it was the "fourth watch of the night," or about three in the morning. When they first saw Jesus walking on the water, they thought it was a spirit (Mark 6:49) and were afraid (Matt. 14:26; John 6:19). Each of the gospel writers records the same message from Jesus: "It is I; don't be afraid." The phrase *ego eimi* is once again employed. It is used to identify the one whom the disciples saw: "Don't be afraid; I AM." Whether or not John intended to focus on Jesus' divinity through the use of this phrase, we may not know, but given the context in which it is written, I believe it is certainly appropriate. Who else could command such power over nature than He who created it? Who else could calm the storm as easily as He calmed the hearts of these seasoned fishermen?

"Don't be afraid; I AM."

As Leon Morris states, "The darkness was not too deep, the waves too high, or the sea too wide for Jesus to calm the fears of His disciples."[12] I AM had come to them, and they were no longer afraid. Mark tells us that when Jesus entered the boat, the wind ceased, and the disciples were "completely amazed" (6:51). John adds, "Then they were willing to take him into the boat, and *immediately* the boat reached the shore where they were headed" (6:21, italics mine).

The disciples struggled for hours against a wind that was "contrary" (Mark 6:48 KJV). This paints a vivid picture in itself. Other words for *contrary* are *hostile*, *adverse*, and *opposing*. In other words, the disciples were not making a lot of progress. Jesus came onto the scene, calmed the wind, and immediately the boat was at land with all occupants safe and sound. Jesus' words "I am" were not empty words spoken by an egocentric man vying for the loyalty of some fishermen. I believe the voice that spoke to them over the sound of the wind and waves was the same voice that spoke to Moses out of the burning bush, and divine authority accompanied His words: "The wind died down" (Mark 6:51) and "immediately the boat reached the shore" (John 6:21). Fredrikson reminds us that what Jesus did was because of who He is, and that He will be all that "It is I" (v. 20) can mean.[13]

In the Garden

The third and last statement of identity is located in John 18:5. The backdrop for this statement is a garden (v. 1). Luke identifies this place as the Mount of Olives, and Matthew further identifies it as the Garden of Gethsemane. They had met in an upper room for the Passover meal, and Jesus had washed the disciples' feet. He had talked to them about hope (chapter 14), about love (chapter 15), about how their grief would turn to joy (chapter 16), and then talked with His Father (chapter 17). Now Jesus led His disciples, minus Judas, into a garden to pray. How long they were there, we are not told, but Jesus' prayer is recorded in Matthew 26:39, Mark 14:36, and Luke 22:42.

John focuses more on the events that would happen next. He tells us that while they were there, a band of men from the chief priests and Pharisees, led by Judas, entered the garden. Matthew and Mark add that it was a "crowd with swords and clubs" (Matt. 26:47; Mark 14:43). Some have suggested that there were as many as six hundred men, a combination of Roman soldiers and Jewish officials.[14] A. Plummer writes, "There is a suppressed journey irony in the details of this verse: all this force against one; against one who intended no resistance; against one who with one word could have swept them all away."[15] The encounter with this mob did not take Jesus by surprise. We read in verse 4, "Jesus, knowing all that was going to happen to Him, went out and asked them." He did not wait for them to approach Him. He went to them and asked a simple question: "Who is it you want?" Which one actually did the speaking, we are not told, possibly the leader of the Roman soldiers. The answer they gave was, "Jesus of Nazareth," to which Jesus responded, *"Ego eimi"* (I AM). Here, "Jesus of Nazareth" supplies the predicate, and Jesus' response is one of identification. However, with what is recorded next, one must wonder if Jesus meant more by His use of *ego eimi* than simple identification.

"When Jesus said, "I am he," they drew back and fell to the ground" (v. 6). Bruce agrees with a double interpretation of *ego eimi* here. "This can be understood on two levels. 'I am he' is used in an ordinary way; 'I am he, the one you seek.' But it can also be used in a more powerful way; the equivalent of the God of Israel's self-identifying, affirmation 'I am he' or simply put, 'I AM.'"[16]

The psalmist gives us a glimpse of this scene: "When evil men advance against me to devour my flesh, when my enemies and my foes attack me, they will stumble and fall back" (Ps. 27:2). At the words of Jesus, *ego eimi*, they could no longer stand in His presence. A second time Jesus asked them, "Who is it you want?" and a second time they answered, "Jesus of Nazareth." Once again Jesus announced *ego eimi* (I AM), but this time added, "If you are looking for me, then let these men go." Jesus allowed them to take Him, on condition they let the disciples go. Even here the words of Jesus back in John 10:18 are seen. Talking about His life, Jesus stated, "No man takes it from me, but I lay it down of my own accord." Standing face-to-face with one who possessed such boldness, such moral grandeur, one who commanded such authority, these men could only move when given permission to do so.

"No one ever spoke like this man does."

This passage is reminiscent of an earlier account when the Pharisees and the chief priests sent officers to take Jesus (John 7:32). In verse 46, the officers returned empty-handed to those who sent them and were asked why they had not taken Jesus, to which they responded, "No one ever spoke like this man does." Jesus, however, was no ordinary man. Here, as in other places, He made a claim that no other could make; He identified Himself as I AM, the eternal God.

Chapter 3

DIALOGUE WITH THE JEWS

We next turn our attention to the absolute use of the phrase "I AM." Here we will discover that Jesus' self-disclosure only became stronger and more intense. He had dealt with the controversy concerning the woman taken in adultery (John 8:1–11), identified Himself as the "light of the world," which we will look at in a later chapter (8:12), and now revealed to all that He was going away (v. 21). Wherever Jesus ministered, there were those whose sole purpose for being there was to challenge His statements or actions. In Matthew 9:1–8, we read where Jesus healed a paralytic. Instead of initially telling the man to stand up, pick up his mat, and go home, which He did say in verse 6, Jesus said, "Take heart, son; your sins are forgiven" (v. 2). The teachers of the Law refused to focus on the fact that the paralyzed man did what Jesus said—he stood up. Instead, they focused on His words, "your sins are forgiven," and accused Jesus of blasphemy. After setting free a man possessed by demons, Jesus was accused of casting out demons by the power of Satan (Matt. 9:35). Sitting at a banquet held by Levi, one of the Twelve, He was criticized for eating and drinking with sinners (Luke 5:30).

In Luke 20, Jesus' authority was again challenged when He was questioned about the legality of paying taxes to Caesar (Luke 20:21). Along with the multitudes that longed to hear His teachings and witness His miracles, there were those who sought any excuse to find blame. As we turn to Jesus' next "I am" statement, we discover that this discourse is no different.

"You will die in your sin."

"I am going away, and you will look for me, and you will die in your sin. Where I go, you cannot come" (8:21). How beautiful are Fredrikson's comments on this verse: "He is going away! Leaving this world beneath, returning to the Father by way of the cross and the resurrection. It is an infinite journey that cannot be measured by earthly standards. These hostile listeners will seek for Him after He is gone but it will be a search of despair, for they cannot come where He is."[1]

Jesus introduced this section with a statement of departure. Such a statement brought about a prophetic response: "Will he kill himself?" (v. 22). Jesus' death on the cross was a voluntary act. As was stated above, no one could take His life, but He would lay it down (John 10:18). Jesus drew a contrast between Himself and those He was speaking to. They were from beneath; He was from above. They were from this world; He was not. The result of this truth was they would die in their sin. This phrase is repeated three times in this discourse.

The apostle Paul declares that "the wages of sin is death" (Rom. 6:23). We are told by the writer of Hebrews, "A man is destined to die once and after that to face judgment" (9:27). All will come to physical death, whether righteous or unrighteous, but to die in our sins is to take those sins with us to judgment. Men need not be lost to heaven, but if they are, it's because they "do not believe that I am the one I claim to be." The results are final: "You will indeed die in your sin" (v. 24). Literally, Jesus was saying that unless they believed He was the I AM, they had no way of escaping the penalty of their sins.

Leon Morris states, "The personal pronoun in Greek is not used the way we use it. The form of verb tells us sufficiently what the subject is. But where God is the speaker, the pronoun is used. The emphatic way of speaking was seen as suitable when a divine person is doing the speaking."[2] To reject Jesus as I AM was to reject God and therefore forfeit their souls. The result of their not believing Jesus' claim to be the I AM substantiated His claim. They would "die in their sin." Who else but God could make such a claim and bring about such a judgment? Man, even a great and powerful man, could not affect the penalty of another man's sin. However, those hearing Jesus' words could avoid such a judgment if they were to accept who He claimed to be. Jesus provided a way of escape. The Jews' next question, "Who are you?" was characteristic of their continued ignorance of Jesus' true identity. "Just what I have been claiming all along" (v. 25). Jesus' message had not changed; neither had their unbelief.

He then said, "When you have lifted up the Son of man, then you will know that I am the one I claim to be" (v. 28). Again, as in verse 24, this can literally read, "Then you will know that I AM." This speaks to the exaltation of Christ by way of the cross. Jesus spoke early in His ministry to a Pharisee named Nicodemus (John 3), and during that conversation Jesus said, "Just as Moses lifted up the snake in the desert, so the Son of man must be lifted up, that everyone who believes in him may have eternal life" (vv. 14–15). Numbers 21:4–8 tells the account that Jesus was speaking about. The Israelites grew impatient and "spoke against God and against Moses," and the judgment they faced was "venomous snakes" that God sent into the camp. Moses was instructed to make a bronze snake and place it on a pole. All those who were bitten were to look at the snake, and they would live. I wonder how many stood there and said, "Hmm, Moses says we have to look on that stupid serpent if we want to live. Well, I'm just not going to look!" Well, I suppose we will never know if that happened or not, but one thing we can know is that this event was a foreshadowing of the cross. Jesus would be placed upon a cross and lifted up. All who looked to Him in faith would live forever.

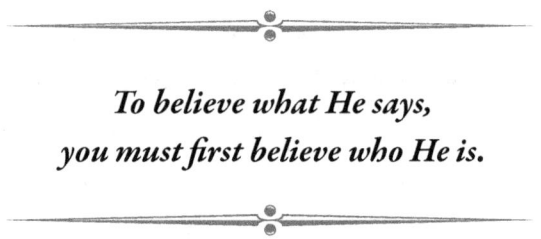

To believe what He says, you must first believe who He is.

This was the message that Jesus was giving them; in fact, His whole conversation with the Jews in this section was to declare the validity of His testimony. To believe what He said, they had to first believe who He was, and it was this point they were unwilling to accept. They had already identified who Jesus was in their eyes: "Is this not Jesus, the son of Joseph, whose father and mother we know?" (John 6:42). He told the Jews that once He was crucified, they would know His real identity. Fredrikson once again paints a vivid picture in his description of this passage that also has a ring of Zechariah 12:10 in it: "They will look on me, the one they have pierced":

> These antagonists will come to know who He is in a strangely unexpected way. It is when they "lift up the Son

of Man," arranging for His shameful crucifixion, that they will know He is the Son of Man, the One who has been sent by the Father, the I AM, who has always been with the Father. Even in the act of dying, He will be pleasing the Father who has never left Him. What an incredible paradox that in the very attempt to get rid of Jesus, these angry men will end up discovering whom it is they have killed! But it will be too late!³

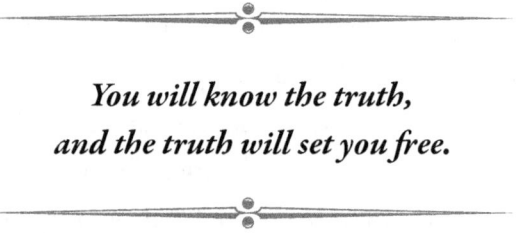

***You will know the truth,
and the truth will set you free.***

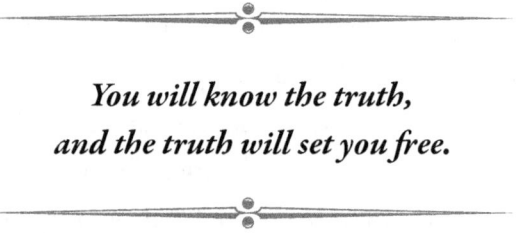

This conversation with the Jews was far from over. Jesus' next statement also drew quite a reaction from His audience. We are told that Jesus directed His words toward those who believed on Him (v. 31). Whether this means that His audience had changed by virtue of the nonbelievers leaving or that Jesus simply focused His attention on those who were responding to His words is not made clear. One also wonders how deep their belief was and how long it would last. Nevertheless, Jesus said, "If you hold to my teaching, you are really my disciples. Then you will know the truth, and the truth will set you free."

A life of freedom was surely something they would be interested in. As children, they had been taught about their forefathers going into slavery and how God heard their cries for help and sent Moses to lead them out of Egypt. They learned how God plagued Egypt until finally the death angel destroyed the firstborn throughout the land of Egypt, with the exception of the Israelites who applied the blood of a lamb to their doorposts (Exodus 11–12). It was here that Passover, which they celebrated every year, was born. They recited how Moses led their fathers to a land they could call their own, a land "flowing with milk and honey" (Ex. 3:8).

They were well versed in the history of their fathers, in the glory of the days of King David and King Solomon. They also knew the bitter stories of how their fathers sinned and were taken into captivity. The struggle for freedom had been with the Jews ever since. However, instead of creating a spark of hope, Jesus' statement only brought back a defensive response. They claimed their heritage in Abraham, and as such, they were never in bondage (v. 33). In today's language, we would say they were living in denial. They needed only to look around them to see the Roman soldiers that occupied Jerusalem. It was true that they lived outwardly in a measure of freedom, as much as the Roman government would allow them. They could earn a living, worship as they pleased, and even travel without approval. If they paid their taxes and didn't cause trouble, Rome was content. Yet the freedom Jesus talked about had nothing to do with the rule of Rome, but the rule of sin. Those who lived in sin were the slaves of sin. For one to be a slave, he must first have a master. Jesus was saying that sin was their master and ultimately is the master of all who have not received Jesus as Savior.

"If anyone keeps my word, he will never see death."

Their discussion turned hostile when Jesus declared that those who keep His word will never see death (v. 51). "Now we know that you are demon possessed" (v. 52). Somewhere through the conversation, their belief appears to have vanished. The words of Jesus must have seemed farfetched. Not die? Once again, they appealed to the life of Abraham. There was no greater man in the eyes of the Jews than their ancestor Abraham. He was not only the father of their nation, but he was "God's friend" (Isa. 41:8). Certainly, if anyone could have avoided death, it was he, but Abraham did die. They then added the prophets to their list, men who had been guided by God to deliver messages to kings. Yet they also were dead. All of Israel's great heroes were dead. How could Jesus make such a statement? Was He greater than their father Abraham?

Jesus did not answer their question right away; instead, He pointed out that though they spoke of God, they really had no knowledge of Him at all. What they had was an illusion built upon religious ideas that made them feel comfortable—not too unlike a lot of people today. Yet Jesus said to them, "You do not know him" (v. 55), referring to the Father. Up to this point, it was the people who continued to bring up Abraham to support their arguments; now Jesus took His turn using the patriarch: "Your father Abraham rejoiced to see my day: and he saw it and was glad." Such a statement puzzled the Jews. How could Abraham have seen Jesus' day, and how could he have rejoiced in it? Arthur Pink gives a threefold answer:

> First, Abraham saw the day of Christ by faith in the promises of God (Heb. 11:13). Second, Abraham saw the day of Christ in type. In offering Isaac on the altar and receiving him back alive from a figurative death, he foreshadowed the Savior's death and resurrection. Third, he saw it through a special revelation.[4]

The "special revelation" that Pink speaks of is his belief that God revealed more to the Old Testament saints than what is recorded. Be that as it may, the final proof that Abraham saw Jesus' day lies in the words of Christ Himself: "Your father Abraham rejoiced at the thought of seeing my day; he saw it and was glad." Since the promise given to Abraham in Genesis 12 stated that he would become a great nation and that all the world would be blessed through him, the birth of Isaac in his old age became the first symbol of the fulfillment of this promise. Receiving Isaac back from the dead—for surely Abraham would have killed him if God had not intervened—was, as Pink states, a foreshadowing of Christ's atonement.

On the defensive again, they responded to Jesus' statement by focusing on His physical age: "You are not yet fifty years old, and you have seen Abraham!" (v. 57). Some authors tend to get sidetracked here by trying to figure out why the Jews used the age of fifty when tradition puts Jesus at the age of thirty. The truth is, had Jesus been the physical age of one hundred, He would still have been too young to have known Abraham in the flesh. The point that they were making is that Jesus was much too young to have lived when Abraham did. Jesus' statement went much deeper than the crowd could comprehend. His answer began with "I tell you the truth."

"Before Abraham was, I AM."

This marked the statement He was about to make with emphasis. It was like a loud proclamation that said, "Listen to what I am about to say." He then went on to contrast Abraham's life with His own: "Before Abraham was born, I am!" John's gospel begins by speaking of the pre-existence of the Word (1:1–14). Here, Christ's pre-existence is brought out in a more striking fashion. Jesus' statement here can only mean a claim to deity. "Was born" implies a condition of existence. There was a time when Abraham was not. He was mortal and therefore is referred to by "was." I AM implies continued existence. Jesus is immortal and eternal and therefore can be referred to as I AM. Jesus was asserting that at the time Abraham was born, He was already on the scene. None but God could make such a claim. Either Jesus was suffering from delusions of grandeur, or He rightly identified Himself as the eternal God. Donald Macleod writes, "The present tense is remarkable, both because it emphasizes the ageless open-endedness of Christ's existence, and because it brings out the continuity between his incarnate life and his pre-incarnate past."[5]

Jesus' claim did not fall on deaf ears, although His claim was rejected. His words were not just absurd to the crowd standing there, but blasphemous. Their response to His claim demonstrated their lack of understanding of what Jesus was saying. He identified Himself not only as the one who revealed Himself to Moses in the burning bush, but also as the one who spoke to Abraham; that is, the God of Abraham, the God of Isaac, and the God of Jacob. They picked up stones to carry out the punishment for blasphemy as directed by Leviticus 24:16: "Anyone who blasphemes the name of the Lord must be put to death. The entire assembly must stone him." The people would later carry out their wish to kill Him through the crucifixion. After that, they would later put Leviticus 24:16 into practice when they stoned a young man named Stephen, who spoke of seeing the heavens opened and the Son of man standing at the right hand of God (Acts 7:56).

Anger filled the hearts of the Jews, and the death of Jesus was their intention. Once again they had rejected His claim, a claim of divinity that was not just empty words, for as they took up stones to cast at Him,

He passed through their midst. Jesus' time to die had not yet come, so as the eternal I AM, He passed through this angry crowd without a stone being cast. Morris quotes Saint Augustine as he commented on this scene: "As man, He fled from stones; but woe to those from whose stony hearts God has fled."⁶

In the Upper Room

There is one last passage to look at that contains the absolute use of the "I AM" phrase, and the setting is the upper room. The Passover was drawing near, and the disciples had followed Jesus' instructions in obtaining a place where they could eat the Passover meal together. This was also the scene for many of Jesus' teachings and is known by Bible students as the Upper Room Discourse. It was here that the disciples received their greatest lesson in service, as their Master wrapped Himself in a towel, picked up a basin of water, and began to wash their feet. Once this act of loving service was completed, Jesus began to instruct them to serve one another in like fashion. In other words, they were not to put themselves above others, but to be willing to serve others in the Spirit of Christ. He also revealed that one of them would betray Him: "I am not referring to all of you; I know those I have chosen. But this is to fulfill the scripture: 'He who shares my bread has lifted up his heel against me'" (13:18). In verse 11 we read, "For he knew who was going to betray him." In a short time, Judas would leave, and with the taste of the meal still in his mouth and the memory of Jesus washing his feet still in his mind, he would betray the one he had called "Lord."

The disciples did not really understand what Jesus was saying, even when they asked Him who it was that would betray Him and He responded, "It is the one to whom I will give this piece of bread when I have dipped it in the dish." He then dipped the morsel and gave it to Judas, but they still failed to get the connection. John 13:29 reveals the disciples' explanation for Jesus giving Judas the morsel, and then Judas leaving: "Since Judas had charge of the money, some thought Jesus was telling him to buy what was needed for the Feast, or to give something to the poor." They did not understand, but then, Jesus did not tell them so they could understand now, but so that they would understand later when all of what He had been talking about came to pass. And what exactly did He want them to understand—that Judas was the betrayer? Not at all! He made it very clear what He wanted them to believe: "I am telling you now before it happens, so that when it does happen you will believe that I am he" (v. 19). Once again, the "he" was not present, and the *ego eimi* can only be understood as a reference to Jesus' deity. Yet I believe that Jesus was doing more than asserting His rightful claim as I AM. His true identity was the only thing that would sustain this band of followers through the dark trials they would endure in the next few days. This Jesus, for whom they had left all to follow, would soon be arrested and hung on a cross.

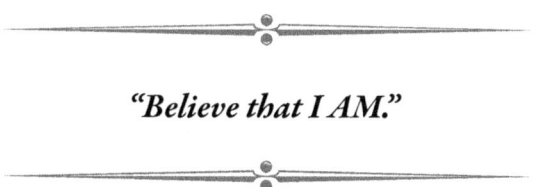

"Believe that I AM."

The Messiah that they believed had come to set them free from outward slavery would make the supreme sacrifice that would set them free from inward slavery. Their master and their friend, whom they witnessed bring others to life, would die before their very eyes. How could they survive such a devastating blow? Jesus' words were meant to comfort them, for no matter how dark the next few days would become, He would always be I AM. Such a comfort reaches down to us even today. We may not always understand what happens or why we must face the difficulties life throws at us, but one truth we can cling to through any storm is that Jesus Christ, the Son of the Living God, is always present. We are not alone in the darkness, and as Psalm 139:12 states, "Even the darkness will not be dark to you; the night will shine like the day, for the darkness is as light to you."

Chapter 4

I AM THE BREAD OF LIFE

The third and final use of the phrase "I AM" as seen in the gospel of John will lead us to some of the most beautiful pictures that can be painted with words. Here the *ego eimi* is used with a predicate and a direct article. These seven statements are the traditionally known "I AM" statements. They have been taught to children in Sunday school lessons and in vacation Bible school songs. These statements identify Jesus in several common images, yet once spoken by Jesus, these images could never again be viewed in the same manner.

The background for this first image was the feeding of the five thousand. Jesus had sent the people away and went up into the mountain to pray, as was discussed in an earlier "I AM" statement. When the people did not find Jesus and discovered He had gone across to the other side of the lake, they followed Him to Capernaum. Once they found Him, they asked when He had gotten there. Jesus saw through their true motives and responded not to their question, but to their hearts: "I tell you the truth, you are looking for me, not because you saw miraculous signs but because you ate the loaves and had your fill" (6:26). The people were hungry again, and perhaps they thought they could get another free meal. Bishop Sheen shares his insight about this encounter: "They had not taken the miracle as a sign of His Divinity; they were looking *for* Him, instead of *to* Him."[1]

Jesus next drew a contrast between the nourishment that perishes and that which endures to everlasting life. He was trying to take them from a physical understanding to a spiritual one, from the temporal to the eternal. He continued His message to them by saying, "Do not work for food that spoils, but for food that endures to eternal life, which the Son of Man will give you" (6:27). Jesus was not scorning their necessity to obtain physical food to nourish them; rather, He was identifying an earthly system that will pass away. To focus one's attention solely on those needs that are physical is to disregard man's greatest need. The gospel writer Mark records Jesus' words on this topic: "What good is it for a man to gain the whole world and forfeit his soul?" (Mark 8:36).

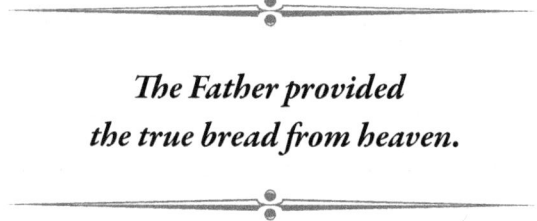

The Father provided the true bread from heaven.

Not content with what they had already seen, they asked for a sign. They had totally put the miracle of the bread and fishes out of their minds. Just the day before, they witnessed five thousand men, plus women and children, eat their fill from five loaves of bread and two small fishes (6:8). Still they were not convinced, so they sought for a sign, perhaps another miracle. Thinking again of their physical needs, they pointed to the manna, which they wrongly attributed to Moses. Jesus corrected their mistaken notion and gave credit where credit was due. It was the Father who had provided manna from heaven for Moses and the Israelites, and it was the Father who had provided these Jews with "the true bread from heaven" (v. 32).

This is the third Old Testament example that Jesus used to symbolize Himself. The first is found in John 1:51, where He likened Himself to the ladder that Jacob saw, thus revealing Himself as the mediator between God and man (Gen. 28:12). The second time was during His discussion with Nicodemus (John 3:14), where He identified Himself with the bronze serpent that Moses lifted up (Num. 21:9), revealing His ability to save those who look to Him. Now on this third occasion, He identified Himself as the true bread from heaven of which the manna was a shadow.[2]

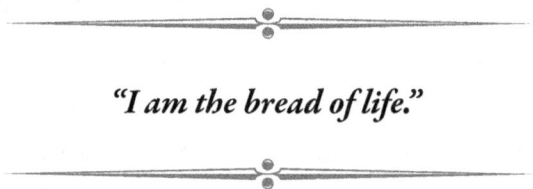

"I am the bread of life."

The response of the people was very similar to that of the woman at the well who said to Jesus, "Sir, give me this water so that I won't get thirsty" (John 4:15). Here, the people responded, "Sir... from now on give us this bread" (John 6:34). In both cases, they were looking for Jesus to supply a physical need that they had been forced to meet themselves. Yet to each, Jesus was revealing Himself, not as a means of physical life, but of spiritual and therefore eternal life. The words spoken by Jesus to the devil during His temptation in the desert were as true for these Jews as they were for Jesus: "Man does not live by bread alone, but on every word that comes from the mouth of God" (Matt. 4:4). They had that same choice, but they were still focused on physical bread instead of the words that were coming out of the mouth of God.

What had been hidden to them in sign and symbol was about to be declared: "I am the bread of life. He who comes to me will never go hungry, and he who believes in me will never be thirsty" (John 6:35). The manna provided to Moses and the Israelites was temporary nourishment. If left overnight, it would rot (Ex. 16:19–20). It satisfied their physical need only and had to be collected every day. Once the Israelites entered Canaan, the manna ceased entirely (Josh. 5:12). The bread that Jesus was giving would be given once to meet man's needs forever.

The people's response to all of this was similar to their forefathers' response in the desert—they murmured. Like father, like son! They referred to Jesus' earthly parents, Joseph and Mary. The crowd knew them; perhaps some of them actually remembered seeing Jesus when He was a child. How could this man say He had come down from heaven? Making a transition from that of earthly parents, Jesus drew their attention to His Heavenly Father. It was He who had sent this "heavenly bread." Once again, Jesus affirmed His role in the Father's plan: "For I have come down from heaven not to do my will but to do the will of him who sent me" (6:38). He reminded them that their fathers who ate the manna all died. The bread they ate could sustain only physical life. Partaking of the bread of which Jesus spoke, they would never die.

Leon Morris comments on this passage, "When man's deepest need has been satisfied, he is forever delivered from the emptiness that is part of the worldly system."[3] As Saint Augustine said in his famous prayer, "Thou hast made us for Thyself and our hearts are restless till they rest in Thee." Such was the case of these to whom Jesus addressed these words: "I am the living bread which came down from heaven." Four times in this chapter, Jesus identified Himself as bread: "I am the bread of life" (6:35), "I am the bread that came down from heaven" (6:41), "I am the bread of life" (6:48), and "I am the living bread" (6:51).

Three thoughts come from these passages. First, Jesus is the source of life. As bread (food) is necessary to sustain physical life, so Jesus is necessary to sustain spiritual life. Second, the origin of this bread is from above. While the people thought they knew where Jesus came from, they failed to look further than Nazareth. Third, this bread from heaven was living bread; not because He was born from Mary in a Bethlehem stable, but because He is the eternal I AM.

If the people had difficulty swallowing Jesus' claims up to this point, they were about to choke on His next comment: "I am the living bread that came down from heaven. If anyone eats of this bread, he will live forever. This bread is my flesh, which I will give for the life of the world" (6:51). Remember, this whole discourse came the day after Jesus had fed the five thousand. It was no accident that Jesus chose this time to reveal Himself as bread. They had already eaten physically of the bread He had provided, and in this miracle we find a foreshadowing of the cross. As the people sat down, the bread was broken before them. Each one of them had to receive the bread and then consume it, and when they had done that, they were filled. Soon Jesus would hang on a cross, broken before them all. However, this time it would not be all who would be filled, but only those who put their faith in Christ. They would have to receive Him themselves and consume Christ into every aspect of their lives, not as a part of a religious ceremony, but as Lord of their lives.

I believe it was this that the writer of Proverbs meant when he wrote, "Trust in the LORD with all your heart and lean not on your own understanding; in all your ways acknowledge him, and he will make your paths straight" (3:5–6). As the five loaves and two fishes were sufficient to feed such a large host of people until they were filled, so Jesus would fill their lives with His Spirit, and His grace would be sufficient for all their needs. The apostle Paul wrote about the sufficiency he had found in Christ: "For if, by the trespass of the one man, Adam, death reigned through that one man, how much more will those who receive God's abundant provision of grace and of the gift of righteousness reign in life by the one man, Jesus Christ" (Rom. 5:17). As the Bread of Life, Jesus said He was the source, the only source, of man's spiritual nourishment.

"He who has the Son has life."

Continuing to stumble over the physical realm, those who heard Jesus came no closer to grasping the truth of His words than they had earlier: "How can this man give us his flesh to eat?" (6:52). Jesus corrected their assumption that He was a mere man: "I tell you the truth unless you eat the flesh of the Son of Man and drink his blood, you have no life in you" (6:53). Perhaps John was thinking of this occasion when he wrote in 1 John 5:12, "He who has the Son has life; and he who does not have the Son of God does not have life."

I remember reading on a church sign, "Some people are so earthly minded they are no heavenly good." Jesus' audience would have fit that slogan, saying, "This is a hard teaching. Who can accept it?" (John 6:60). The truth can be hard to take, especially for those who would seek an easier way. Even today there are scores of people who would seek an easier way than a full commitment to the Lord Jesus Christ. They place their hope for redemption on the church they attend, the denomination they are a part of, or perhaps the good deeds they perform. Yet it is all in vain. Jesus gives no exception; to possess life, we must consume Him.

***"The words I have spoken to you
are spirit, and they are life."***

It was not the saying that was hard; it was their hearts. Sadly, Jesus watched as many walked away, unable to understand that the words He was speaking were not focused on the physical realm, but on the spiritual. He said in 6:63, "The Spirit gives life; the flesh counts for nothing. The words I have spoken to you are spirit and they are life." Bishop Sheen makes an excellent comparison here: "As man died spiritually by physically eating in the Garden of Eden, so he would live again spiritually through eating the fruit of the Tree of Life."[4] The reference he makes to this Tree of Life is none other than Jesus Christ, the Bread of Life, given by the Father for the life of the world (6:33).

Chapter 5

I AM THE LIGHT OF THE WORLD

From the discussion of bread, we travel to the temple, where Jesus had gone early in the morning. As He sat down, people gathered around Him, which seems to have been the norm. Wherever Jesus was, a crowd surely developed. Whether they came in hope of seeing a miracle, or perhaps to be one, or to listen to His teaching—whatever their reason—the people came. When Jesus spoke again to the people, He said, "I am the light of the world. Whoever follows me will never walk in darkness, but will have the light of life" (John 8:12). He repeated the message that He is the light of the world in John 9:5. Light and darkness are two concepts man knows quite well. It is a fundamental feature of human existence.

Day and night, light and shadows make up the world in which we live. Light can be a place of comfort and security, such as how a child crying out in the night feels when the light is turned on. To some, however, light becomes a means of exposing their evil deeds (John 3:20). Darkness may fall around a family enjoying an evening meal and yet cover the movements of a thief. The image of light is scattered throughout the Bible and would have been known by His Jewish listeners. Isaiah writes, "Arise, shine; for your light has come, and the glory of the Lord rises upon you"

(Isa. 60:1), and then again in 60:3, "Nations will come to your light, and kings to the brightness of your dawn." Isaiah continues this theme later in this chapter: "The sun will no more be your light by day, nor will the brightness of the moon shine on you, for the LORD will be your everlasting light" (v. 19). The psalmist also uses the "light" imagery: "The LORD is my light and my salvation; whom shall I fear?" (27:1), and "Your word is a lamp to my feet, and a light for my path" (119:105).

Darkness is defined as the absence of light, and there are many references to darkness in Scripture as well. For our purposes here, however, we will focus on the light. It should be mentioned, though, that if light is associated with life (1:4), then darkness could only suggest death, physical and spiritual. This is the picture that is painted in the epics of Homer, which were a part of Greek education even through the New Testament period.[1] One who was dying was depicted as "that hateful darkness got a hold of him," or "darkness enfolded his eyes."[2] Jesus' announcement to be the "light of the world" (John 8:12) can only mean that the world was in darkness. One who is not in darkness does not need a light. Yet man need not stay in darkness, for Jesus said, "He that followeth me shall not walk in darkness" (John 8:12 KJV). Jesus came into the world not only to provide light, but also to *be* the light.

When Mary and Joseph took Jesus to the temple after the allotted time as described in the Law, a man named Simeon, who we are told was waiting for the "consolation of Israel" (Luke 2:52), took Jesus in his arms and blessed God, saying, "Sovereign Lord, as you have promised, you may now dismiss your servant in peace. For my eyes have seen your salvation, which you have prepared in the sight of all people, a light for revelation to the Gentiles and for glory to your people Israel" (Luke 2:29–32). Those who reject Him, preferring to stay in darkness, condemn themselves.

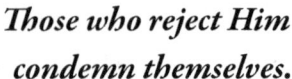

Those who reject Him condemn themselves.

The setting for Jesus' proclamation is also interesting, as well as the time frame. All that surrounded Jesus spoke to the necessity of light. We are told in John 8:20 that He was in the treasury of the temple, which was the Court of the Women. This was the most public part of the temple.[3] The time corresponded with the Feast of Tabernacles, a time when the golden candelabras were lit. Throughout the night, young men from priestly families would pour oil into the bowls of the candelabras so that they would burn continuously through the feast.[4]

Vincent even suggests that the candelabras were a figure of the Messiah, that according to tradition, light was one of the names for the Messiah.[5] Such scriptures as Isaiah 9:2; 60:1; Malachi 4:2; and Luke 2:32 back up such claims. The Feast of Tabernacles commemorates the pillar of cloud by day and pillar of fire by night that led Israel as they left Egypt. The pillar of fire by night provided them with light (Ex. 13:21), as well as with a sense of safety. Not many in their right mind would attack such a vast number of people in the desert, especially with a pillar of fire watching over them.

Light is consistent with His nature.

Light became a symbol of God's presence (Ps. 27:1; 43:3; Isa. 2:5; 60:20; Micah 7:8). This is the scenery that Jesus chose to make such a bold statement. Yet light is consistent with His nature. Light possesses many qualities that make it important to man's way of life, and in each of these qualities, Jesus operates.

Light reveals. Anyone who has ever gotten up in the middle of the night and attempted to make their way in the dark understands the importance of the light to reveal obstacles in their path. It is light that enables us to drive at night, not only revealing anything that might be in the road, but revealing to others that we are on the road. As the light, Jesus sought to reveal to the people the way out of the darkness that gripped their lives. Yet for this same reason, people avoid the light. They do not want their deeds to be revealed (John 3:19). As the light, Jesus also reveals the Father to us. He said in John 7:16, "My teaching is not my own. It comes from him who sent me."

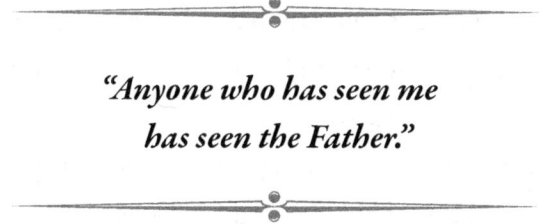

"Anyone who has seen me has seen the Father."

In John 8:28, Jesus said, "I do nothing on my own but speak just what the Father has taught me," and again in 8:38, "I am telling you what I have seen in the Father's presence." Philip said much later in 14:8, "Lord, show us the Father, and that will be enough for us." Jesus responded to Philip's statement with, "Anyone who has seen me has seen the Father" (John 14:8–9). Both through Jesus' words and His actions, the Father is revealed.

Light illuminates. With the flip of a switch, a darkened room is flooded with light. Yet the term *illuminate* means more than just "to give light." Webster defines it as "to provide with understanding." In Romans

1:21, Paul stated that because men did not glorify or thank God, but instead became vain, proud thinkers, their minds became darkened. The darkness that gripped their hearts and minds only led them farther into sin and farther from God. Looking down from the cross, Jesus prayed, "Father, forgive them, for they do not know what they are doing" (Luke 23:34). Their hearts were darkened. Without light, they simply couldn't understand the extent of their actions. Jesus, as the Light of the World, illuminates man's understanding about sin and its consequences that would not only cause pain in this life, but also mean eternal separation from God. He told the crowd that gathered around Him earlier, and He tells us through His Word, that they who commit sin are the slaves of sin. He came to earth to settle the sin problem, and as the light, He provides the illumination man needs to grasp this truth. The fullest extent of His illumination will be experienced in heaven. Revelation 22:5 states, "There will be no more night. They will not need the light of a lamp or the light of the sun, for the Lord God will give them light." His very presence will be sufficient to light all of heaven.

Light reflects. I remember as a young boy looking at the night sky during a full moon, thinking how bright it looked yet wondering why I could not see it during the day. I simply did not know then that the moon has no light of its own; it reflects the sun's light. George Stewart writes, "Jesus provides an atmosphere for reflection in which men can evaluate not only their own lives, but the true values of life. He furnished a basis for the comparison of temporary and permanent values."[6] We live in a society today that has lowered its values. Life is less precious, purity is scoffed at, lying is acceptable, unfaithfulness is the norm, and violence is the answer to all conflict. Yet these values do not reflect the God of love, but the god of this world.

As followers of Christ, it is His light that should be reflected in our lives.

Through Christ, we are able to distinguish between that which is eternal and that which will pass away. We are able to build our lives on the unshakeable principles of God's Word, not the whims of a secular system. As followers of Christ, it is His light that should be reflected in our lives. Jesus stated in Matthew 5:16, "Let your light shine before men, that they may see your good deeds and praise your Father in heaven." Since we have no light of our own, like the moon, we need to reflect the one who is the Light of the World.

Light protects. Most businesses maintain a well-lit property. The light provides protection against someone trying to break in. As police cars pass by, it is the light that enables them to see if anything is out of the ordinary. The light that Jesus sheds on man's conscience protects him from the attitudes of a darkened world. John writes, "Dear friends, do not believe every spirit, but test the spirits to see whether they are from God, because many false prophets have gone out into the world" (1 John 4:1). They may not be standing on street corners proclaiming their false doctrines, yet there are many false beliefs within our society. Some have their base in secular humanism; others may have on the robes of religious piety, yet their doctrine is as deadly as any poison. Jesus' prayer for His disciples was, "Sanctify them by the truth; your word is truth" (John 17:20). His light also protects us from in-growing selfishness by the brilliance of His love. It was God's light that David asked for in Psalm 139:23–24, "Search me, O God, and know my heart; test me and know my anxious thought.

See if there is any offensive way in me, and lead me in the way everlasting." Jesus is the Light of the World, and in His light we find safety from the attacks without and within.

Light directs. As a young teen, I used to go hunting with my father. It was getting toward dusk one evening, and as we headed home, a large herd of deer ran right across the road in front of us. As my dad stopped the car, I jumped out with rifle in hand and headed up the hill after the herd. With each pumping of my heart, I ran farther away from the road, excited that maybe I would get my first deer. At the top of the hill, I spotted them again, and down the other side I went until I realized that I was surrounded by darkness. Panic set in, and as I started back, even my footprints were no longer visible. Without any light, I had no way of knowing which way I was going. As I made it to the top of the hill, I saw lights in the distance and followed them. They brought me safely back to the road; it was then I discovered that the lights were the headlights of my dad's car. He had been driving back and forth trying to show me the way. Jesus is the light that breaks through the darkness of sin and shows the direction to go. Those who follow Him will never have to walk in darkness again. Holman Hunt, on his canvas *The Light of the World* portrays Jesus knocking at a door with a lantern in His hand, knocking patiently and respectfully, with no intention of forcing His way inside. The door that Jesus is knocking on has no handle on the outside. It can be opened only from within, by us, and with an opened door in comes the Light of the World.

Jesus said, "I am the light of the world" and then proceeded to open the eyes of a man born blind. What He did physically for this man, He sought to do spiritually for the people of that day, and still seeks to open eyes today, but they refused. Will we? As the Light of the World, Jesus seeks to lead mankind out of his sin and into the light of God's grace and glory.

Chapter 6

I AM THE DOOR

*J*esus went from one common image, light, to another common image, that of a door. Yet this was not just any door, but the door to a sheep pen. Sheep herding was a popular occupation in Palestine. Many of our favorite Bible heroes were at one time shepherds. Each time I read Psalm 23, I think of David, sitting on a hillside with the sheep bedded down for the night and reflecting on himself as one of God's sheep. Knowing the care a shepherd must give his sheep, David understood the love and care of the one he called his Shepherd.

Outside of Jerusalem, as well as in most villages, the shepherd tending his flocks was a common sight. Drawing from this image, Jesus said, "I tell you the truth, the man who does not enter the sheep pen by the gate, but climbs in by some other way, is a thief and a robber" (10:1). As Fredrikson states, "This is not only a tender pastoral teaching, but a stinging indictment of those who profess to be shepherds but are actually thieves and robbers, strangers and hirelings."[1] The Pharisees identified in John 9:40 no doubt fell into the category of thieves and robbers.

The gate, or door, imagery is something that everyone can identify with. In today's society, with all its regulations and building codes, there are a number of doors on every building. Such was not the case in Jesus' day. Most buildings had just one doorway, a place to enter. This was especially true about the sheep pen. Having only one door was for maximum security to protect the sheep. At night the sheep were herded into enclosures where they would be safe from wild animals or thieves.[2] It was the shepherd who entered by the door; others would seek to enter in some other fashion that would conceal their entrance.

"Whoever enters through me will be saved."

Identifying the gate as the only true way to enter, Jesus announced, "I am the gate for the sheep" (John 10:7), and "I am the gate; whoever enters through me will be saved. He will come in and go out, and find pasture" (v. 9). Jesus is the door, which stands in contrast to the "other way" of verse 1. The church of every era has had to deal with those who would disguise themselves as sheep or shepherds in order to take over the flock, claiming to be the way to enter. Names such as Jim Jones and David Koresh come to mind as those who claimed to be the door but were revealed as wolves in sheep's clothing. The true sheep would not follow them.

In Jewish thinking, people entered heaven by a door or gate. This is seen in different Old Testament passages: "the gate of heaven" (Gen. 28:17), "the doors of heaven" (Ps. 78:23), and in Jesus' words, "Make every effort to enter through the narrow door" (Luke 13:24). According to C. K. Barrett, this is a theme that is found in several literary sources from Homer onwards, the thought of heaven situated above the earth with a door between them whereby the Redeemer descends from heaven, and the redeemed ascend.³ By Jesus identifying Himself as the door, the "I AM" is given even more of an emphasis. The two terms go well together, for they both say the same thing. "I AM" identifies Jesus as the eternal God. Although His hearers saw flesh and bones before them, confined within this body of flesh was their creator (John 1:3; Col. 1:15–17). As the door, Jesus is the only access to redemption, and therefore heaven: "Whoever enters through me will be saved" (v. 9).

The door of a Palestinian sheepfold was not the gate, which closed the opening; it was the opening itself.⁴ Arthur Pink writes:

> Each village had a large sheepfold, which was the common property of the native farmers. A wall between ten to twelve feet high protected this sheepfold. When night fell, a number of different shepherds would lead their flocks up to the door of the sheepfold, through which they would pass. The shepherds would leave their flocks in the care of a porter who watched them through the night. At the door of the fold, the porter would lie across the entrance and protect the sheep. In the morning, the shepherds would come to the sheepfold and retrieve their flocks. The porter would allow them entrance, and they would call their sheep. Since the sheep knew their shepherd's voice, they could come to him, and the shepherd would lead them out to pasture.⁵

"I am the door!" Just one step and those on the outside are now safe within. The soul that believes the testimony of Christ at once enters into the presence of God. Phillip Keller even draws a connection between Jesus as the door and the door to which the Hebrews applied blood prior to the great exodus. Blood was applied to the lintel over the doorway and to both doorposts. Anyone passing through the door into the shelter of the house was assured of protection and absolute safety.[6] "I am the gate; whoever enters through me will be saved."

The use of the direct article is also important here. Jesus did not say He was *a* gate, but

the gate. There was only one door in the ark for Noah and his family to go in and find safety,

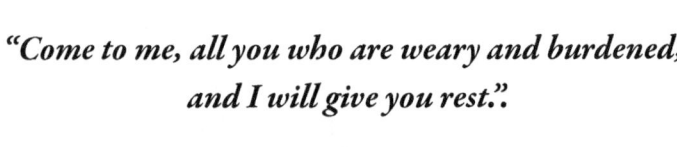

> *"Come to me, all you who are weary and burdened, and I will give you rest."*

only one door existed into the Holy of Holies for the high priest to enter, and there was only one door into the sheepfold—one entrance into heaven. Jesus boldly proclaimed He was that door. Man has sought to find other entrances into God's kingdom. He has tried good works, church membership, and new philosophies ranging from Eastern mysticism to universalism, but to no avail. They are all thieves and robbers seeking to destroy the flock. There is no other way, no other entrance, than Jesus Christ. Man is hopelessly lost unless he enters the fold through the only door God has provided; that is, faith in Christ. He is the door!

As the door, Jesus provides refuge for those who enter. He said in Matthew 11:28, "Come to me, all you who are weary and burdened, and I will give you rest." Later in Matthew 16:18, He said, "I will build my church, and the gates of Hades will not overcome it." He is the door that leads to peace. Jesus told His disciples, "Peace I leave with you; my peace

I give you" (John 14:27). In a world where war seems to be increasing, it is comforting to know that Christ provides a peace that is untouched by the circumstances we face. He is also the door where we enter in and find shelter and safety from a world that has rebelled against God.

He is the door whereby we enter into the Holy of Holies, into the very presence of the Father (John 14:6). He is the door by which we enter into God's fold and find rest, where we can come in and go out and find pasture. Jesus is *the* door. "Salvation is found in no one else, for there is no other name under heaven given to men by which we must be saved" (Acts 4:12). "No one comes to the Father, except through me" (John 14:6). As *the* door, Jesus is the only entrance for man to find safety, and all those who enter can say with David, "Surely goodness and mercy shall follow me all the days of my life, and I shall dwell in the house of the Lord forever" (Ps. 23:6 KJV).

Chapter 7

I AM THE GOOD SHEPHERD

No discussion about the door of the sheep can be carried on for very long without the topic of the shepherd coming up. One of the most beloved portraits I have seen of Jesus displays Him holding a young lamb. John develops this picture through the rest of the chapter. After identifying Himself as the door, Jesus then stated, "I am the good shepherd" (10:11). The concept of a divine shepherd goes back to the Old Testament. The twenty-third psalm begins, "The Lord is my shepherd." In Jeremiah 23:1–3, God condemned the shepherds of Israel, accusing them of "destroying and scattering the sheep of my pasture."

Ezekiel recorded God's words in Ezekiel 34:11: "For this is what the Sovereign Lord says: I myself will search for my sheep, and look after them." In verse 15, He continued, "I myself will tend my sheep and have them to lie down, declares the Sovereign Lord." God revealed in verse 23 that He was sending a shepherd who would feed them: "I will place over them one shepherd, my servant David, and he will tend them." Since at the writing of this verse David was already dead, it is a direct reference to the Messiah.

Matthew 9:27 and 22:42 both make references to Jesus being the "Son of David." Another direct reference is found in Matthew 2:6 as he quotes the prophet Micah: "But you, Bethlehem, in the land of Judah, are by no means least among the rulers of Judah; for out of you will come a ruler who will be the *shepherd* of my people Israel" (italics mine). This messianic promise had been fulfilled in the midst of the people, and though Jesus said, "I am the good shepherd," they could not make the connection. The writer of the letter to the Hebrews, however, drew on this as he wrote his closing remarks: "May the God of peace, who through the blood of the eternal covenant brought back from the dead our Lord Jesus, *that great Shepherd of the sheep*, equip you with everything good for doing his will" (13:20–21, italics mine). In 1 Peter 2:25, Jesus is referred to as "the Shepherd and Overseer of your souls," and later in 5:4, He is called the "Chief Shepherd."

Jesus used the Greek word *kalos* for "good." The word literally means "good, beautiful" and is in contrast to the "idle" shepherds of Zechariah 11:17. Any "good" shepherd will always bear in mind what is best for the flock. Nothing delights a good shepherd more than to know his sheep are in excellent condition. Keller reflects on his own experience as a shepherd:

> My sheep had literally been the recipients of my life. It had been shared with them abundantly and unstintingly. Nothing was ever held back. All that I possessed was in truth poured out unremittingly in order that together we should prosper. The strength of my young body, the keen enthusiasm of my spirit, the energy of my mind, the alertness of my emotions, the thrust and drive of my disposition were all directed to the well-being of my flock. And it showed in abundant measure.[1]

"He calls his own sheep by name."

Jesus said, "I am the good shepherd" (John 10:11), and through the next few verses He identified specific actions that backed up His claim. "He calls his own sheep by name" (v. 3). They are not just a flock of sheep, but each one has a name, a personality, specific needs that the shepherd is aware of. He can tell them apart even if no one else can because he knows his sheep, and they know him.

Dr. Bob Boyd tells a story about his encounter with a group of shepherds in Palestine while researching his book *The Testimony of a Sheep*. Watching a group of shepherds bringing their flocks to Joseph's well near Dothan, where Joseph was sold into slavery by his brothers, he noticed that while the shepherds were chatting, the sheep mingled until about ten different flocks were all mixed together. He was curious how they would ever figure out whose sheep were whose. When one of the shepherds was ready to move, he simply went to the edge of the huge flock and gave a particular call. The sheep would begin to move throughout this massive flock, until all his sheep were together and ready to move. The sheep knew the voice of their shepherd. Amused at this, Dr. Boyd's wife went to the huge flock that remained and gave a loud call of her own, yet not one sheep moved, for "they will never follow a stranger" (v. 5).[2]

Those who know Christ hear His voice because of the unique relationship they have with Him. This is seen at the tomb after the resurrection. Mary had gone to the tomb early in the morning and found the stone had been rolled away (John 20:1–18). She rushed off to tell the disciples that the body of Jesus had been taken. She returned to the tomb with Peter and the "other disciple, the one Jesus loved," whom most scholars believe to be John. The disciples surveyed the surroundings, finding it just as Mary had said, and then returned to their homes, no doubt as perplexed as Mary. She, however, stayed at the tomb, weeping at the entrance. Through her tears, she saw movement in the garden and turned to see a man. Mistaking him for the gardener, Mary called out to him to reveal the location of Jesus' body, if he knew it. With His simple mention of her name, "Mary," she recognized her Lord. The Shepherd had spoken, and Mary, one of His sheep, recognized His voice. The sheep always hear the voice of the Shepherd, and they follow Him.

We read in verse 4, He "goes ahead of them." Our Shepherd does not drive His sheep from the rear; He goes ahead and leads. What a beautiful image this portrays! A shepherd leads his flock, discovering green pastures for them to feed on, clear streams of refreshing water, and valleys of safety to rest. With Jesus in the lead, He is able to watch for the places of danger that could cause His sheep to get caught or injured. He is able to determine if the slope is too steep for the sheep or if He needs to lead them through a different path. There are many decisions that He is able to make because He is leading, and the sheep follow the Shepherd. How true this is of our Great Shepherd! As we allow Him to lead us, He sees all the areas of danger that are unseen to us. He knows which path will bring us more into the center of His will, the way that is most beneficial for us. He leads; we must follow.

John continued his description of the Shepherd in verse 10 "I have come that they might have life, and have it to the full." I have pondered this statement in the context it was given, that of the shepherd and his sheep. What is a "full life" to a sheep? A good shepherd provides the best he can for his sheep, for the shepherd is revealed in his sheep. If the sheep are well cared for, taken to the best pastures, kept from the briars that would destroy their wool, and protected from the attack of wild animals, their appearance will reflect that special care, and their care reflects on the shepherd. That is providing life to its fullest for the sheep. Jesus came that we might have life to its fullest as well. He said in Matthew 6:25, "Therefore, I tell you, do not worry about your life, what you will eat or drink; or about your body, what you will wear." He then tells us why in verse 33: "But seek first his kingdom and his righteousness, and all these things will be given to you as well." Jesus provides pastures of spiritual food throughout the Scriptures; He gives "water welling up to eternal life" (John 4:14). As our Shepherd, He is reflected in the lives we live.

"The good shepherd lays down his life for the sheep" (v. 11). In Jesus' own words, "Greater love has no one than this, that he lay down his life for his friends" (John 15:13). Jesus foretold not only His own sacrificial death, but also His resurrection, as seen in 10:17–18: "I lay down my life—only to take it up again. No one takes it from me, but I lay it down of my own accord." Not only did He die for those who called Him friend, but He also said, "*Whoever* enters through me will be saved" (v. 9, italics mine). We are told in verse 14 that He knows His sheep, and His sheep know Him. The Greek word for "know" is *ginosko*, and it expresses more than just mere facts; it implies a relationship of trust and intimacy.

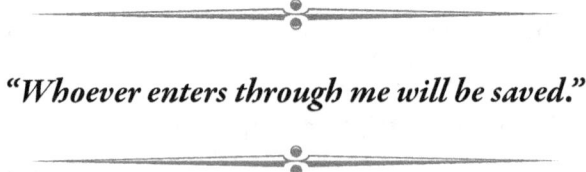

"Whoever enters through me will be saved."

No one spends more time with the sheep than the shepherd, and no one knows them to the extent that the shepherd does. As God's shepherd, Jesus knows His sheep. This in itself provides much comfort to the flock of the redeemed. The shepherd who knows his flock knows which one is more apt to wander. He will know which one is weaker, which one is more resistant to being led, and the one who needs a little extra care. The shepherd knows his sheep so well that he can predict their behavior. Jesus said of Judas, "Have I not chosen you, the Twelve, and one of you is a devil?" (John 6:70). He saw in Zacchaeus what none of the other people saw. Peter denied Him three times, but Jesus saw a different Peter, one who would help provide leadership to a young church. Jesus took the time to stop by a well and talk to a woman that few would have given a second thought to. He saw in her the spark that would set off a revival in a town that desperately needed the truth He had to offer. As the Good Shepherd, He went before them, and He goes before us and leads us to be more productive than we ever could be without Him. The Shepherd knows His sheep, or as Paul told young Timothy in 2 Timothy 2:19, "The Lord knows those who are his." The sheep in turn know they can trust their shepherd, because a stranger they will not follow.

"The Lord knows those who are his."

Arthur Pink brings up an interesting point. He explains that most shepherds were not the owners of the sheep, but the ones to whom the sheep had been entrusted. This is not the same thing as the "hired hand" spoken of in verse 12. The shepherd had a vested interest in the sheep. Examples that he gives are Jacob, Moses, and David, who tended not their own flocks, but their fathers', or in Jacob's and Moses' cases, their fathers-in-law's. This, he says, speaks to Christ as mediator. Jesus was appointed by the Father to act as a shepherd, the one to whom God committed man's redemption.[3] In John 6:36, Jesus stated, "For I have come down from heaven not to do my will but to do the will of him who sent me." When encouraged by His disciples to eat, Jesus told them, "My food . . . is to do the will of him who sent me and to finish his work" (John 4:34). For any shepherd, the work is to bring the sheep safely home.

Pink also points out that the shepherd's voice was associated with special benefits.[4] At one command, the sheep would be led out to pasture or to water. The shepherd had a call that would calm their fears and one that would alert them to danger. With another call, they would stop to rest or be bedded down for the night. When the shepherd spoke, it was always in the sheep's best interests. So it is with Christ. He may speak through His Word or through His Spirit within. He may choose to speak to our hearts through a devotional, a song, a sermon, or a still, small voice. Whether to lead in a specific direction, to calm our fears, or to comfort the brokenhearted, whenever He speaks, it is in His sheep's best interests, and they hear His voice.

Jesus also said there were other sheep that were not a part of the flock of Israel (v. 16). This other flock, the Gentiles, had to be brought to Him, and then He would be the one Shepherd, and we would be one flock. This is also seen in the Great Commission in Matthew 28:19, Luke 24:47, and Acts 1:8. Who else but the Good Shepherd, the divine Son of God, could unite two totally different flocks, a Jewish one and a Gentile one? Even within the Gentile church, there is so much diversity in worship style, doctrinal beliefs, and church governments. Division has been caused over everything from the style of music to the color of the carpet. Yet the promise of our Shepherd is that we will be *one* flock. There will be nothing to divide the flock, for all will follow the Shepherd. In Jesus' claim, "I am the good shepherd," He not only used the phrase *ego eimi* (I AM), but also connected it with an Old Testament image that reveals Him as the Shepherd, not only of Israel, but also of the world. The Shepherd goes before, leading, guiding, and calling us by name. We are His sheep, and as such, we must follow our Shepherd.

As was already stated, it was in Jesus' revelation of Himself as the Good Shepherd that He first mentioned His resurrection. He stated, "The reason my Father loves me is that I lay down my life—only to take it up again. No one takes it from me, but I lay it down and have authority to take it up again" (vv. 17–18). In our next passage, we see that Jesus not only spoke about the resurrection, but also demonstrated His power over death.

Chapter 8

I AM THE RESURRECTION AND LIFE

Chapter 11 of John begins with, "Now a man named Lazarus was sick." We are told that Lazarus lived in Bethany with his two sisters, Mary and Martha. We know from other passages that these three were close friends of Jesus (Matt. 26:7; Luke 10:38; John 12:3). Lazarus had become sick, and his sisters sent word to Jesus, believing that He would come to them and heal their brother. With all the healings that Jesus had performed, surely He would come at their request. Of course, He knew the outcome already and let the disciples know ahead of time that the sickness Lazarus had would not end in his death. I am sure to those hearing this statement, it meant that Lazarus would not die, but Jesus meant that his sickness, and even death, was temporary. He waited two days before heading out for Bethany. This was unlike any of His other healings.

When Jesus prepared to go and heal the centurion's servant, the centurion replied that all Jesus had to do was say the word and his servant would be healed. Jesus commended him for his faith and told him to go, that his servant was healed (Matt. 8:5–13). When faced with ten lepers,

He simply told them to go show themselves to the priests. The healing took place as they went on their way (Luke 17:12–17). This, however, was different. Jesus did nothing for two days and even told His disciples as they finally began their journey toward Bethany, "Lazarus is dead" (v. 14). He had already mentioned in verse 4 that it was for the glory of God that this had happened. It was one more demonstration of not only His authority and power, but also His identity.

Upon reaching the home of Lazarus, Jesus was met by Martha, who stated openly that if He had come sooner, Lazarus would be alive. It almost appears to be a reprimand. She had certainly heard of the miracles of healing Jesus had performed and no doubt witnessed them. She spoke with confidence that had Jesus appeared earlier, Lazarus would still be alive. It is Martha's next statement that seems puzzling. She appears to demonstrate a greater element of faith when she said, "But I know that even now God will give you whatever you ask" (v.22). What she meant is not quite clear, since when it came time for Jesus to perform the miracle that she asked for, she stopped Him, saying, "By this time there is a bad odor, for he has been there four days" (v. 39). Whatever she meant by this statement, one thing is certain: she did not let the death of her brother affect her relationship with Jesus.

Many people through the years have lost faith in God with the loss of a loved one. They seem to cry out within themselves with the words of Martha, that had God been there, their loved one would still be alive. Jesus sought to reassure Martha, as well as each of us today, by saying that her brother would rise again. Death never has the final say. The faith that Martha expressed was a common belief that all Jews shared, except the Sadducees, that a general resurrection would occur. She had the right dogma but failed to see the Person. As the woman at the well voiced a belief in the Messiah but was unable to see that the Messiah was standing before her, so Martha verbalized a belief in the resurrection without realizing the Resurrection stood in front of her in the person of Jesus. "One of the lessons we learn from this," says Arthur Pink, "is that faith does not lie in right theology, but in a Person."[1]

Jesus declared, "I am the resurrection and the life. He who believes in me will live, even though he dies; and whoever lives and believes in me will never die" (v. 25). Jesus first gave glory to the Father, which He stated was for the benefit of those who were standing there so that they might believe God had sent Him. He then proceeded to exercise authority over death.

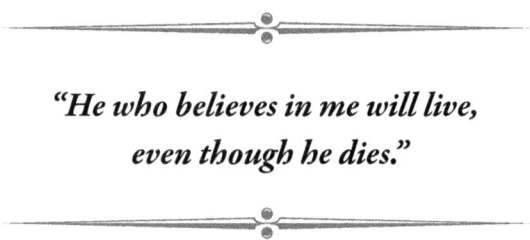

"He who believes in me will live, even though he dies."

It was understood that God alone had the power to give life to the dead, and by exercising that power, He revealed His unity with the Father (5:21). "He who believes in me will live, even though he dies" speaks of Jesus as the *resurrection*. "Whoever lives and believes in me will never die," speaks of Him as the *life*. He said much the same thing in John 5:24: "I tell you the truth, whoever hears my word and believes him who sent me has eternal life and will not be condemned; he has crossed over from death to life."

"I am the resurrection and the life." Both are necessary. Resurrection without the promise of eternal life would be a continuous reincarnation, rising again and again to the same kind of miseries and sufferings we have already faced. Life without the resurrection would cause the reality of Paul's words in 1 Corinthians 15:19: "If only for this life we have hope in

Christ, we are to be pitied more than all men." John Exell writes, "Death is no more death, but resurrection to the fullest life. Christ now gives us life that cannot die. He is the Resurrection, because He is the Life."[2]

It is important also to realize that the life that Jesus is talking about is not separate from the life to come. One does not end at death, and the other begin at resurrection. They are one and the same. Through all our existence there runs one imperishable life. From the moment of conception, we are an eternal soul that has been given a body, a life that will never end. Faith in Christ does not make us immortal; we are immortal from birth. To quote a bumper sticker I once saw, "Everyone will spend eternity *somewhere*!" However, faith in Christ takes away the power of death over us. Sure, we will die physically, but we need not be separated from God for eternity. To the spiritually dead (Eph. 2:1), those who have never received Christ as Savior, Jesus promises to raise them out of their grave of guilt and separation from God to a new life in Christ if they place their trust in Him. The new birth (John 3:3) is a passing from death to life (John 5:24).

The term *dead man walking* was coined for those awaiting execution. No better term could be used to describe those who remain unregenerate. Dead in "trespasses and sins" (Eph. 2:1), they live out their lives without giving thought to the one who can pardon their sin. In John 5:25, Jesus said, "A time is coming, and now has come, when the dead will hear the voice of the Son of God and those who hear will live." This promise of life is given to those who are spiritually dead and respond to the call of Jesus. As the source of life, He provides a life that not even death can tarnish. After proclaiming to be the resurrection and the life, Jesus' words became a reality in Lazarus's life. C. H. Dodd puts verses 25 and 26 in an interesting correlative form (KJV):

> I am the resurrection———he that believeth in me, though he were dead, yet shall he live.
> I am the life ————————whoever liveth and believeth in me shall never die.

He then compares John 5:28 with John 11:17:

> "Those who are in the tombs" 5:28
> "He found Lazarus in the tomb" 11:17

> "Will hear His voice" 5:28
> "He cried with a loud voice, 'Lazarus, come forth'" 11:17

> "And come out" 5:28
> "He that was dead came forth" 11:17[3]

Jesus' claim to be both the resurrection and the life means that all hope for life with God, both in this present time and the future to come, must be viewed through Christ. Any hope for an eternity in the heavenly city prepared for God's people must come from an acceptance of Jesus Christ as Lord of our lives. His divine nature can be seen in His proclamation, "I am the resurrection and the life."

Chapter 9

I AM THE WAY, THE TRUTH, AND THE LIFE

From a town in Bethany, we travel two miles to Jerusalem. It was the Passover season, and Jesus had given instructions to the disciples to obtain a room for them to observe the Passover meal together. Once seated around the table, Jesus began to teach what would be called the Upper Room Discourse. The teachings found in this discourse are unique to John's gospel. In chapter 13, Jesus taught about humility and servanthood through His example of washing the disciples' feet and said that the true sign of greatness is our ability to serve others. In chapter 14, He opened the blinds of heaven that we might get a peek and then stated that He was going before us to prepare things so that we might join Him. It was in response to Thomas's question where we find Jesus' next "I am" statement: "Thomas said to him, 'Lord, we don't know where you are going, so how can we know the way?' Jesus answered, 'I am the way and the truth and the life. No one comes to the Father except through me'" (14:6).

Before sin entered the history of man, Adam enjoyed a threefold relationship with God: he knew Him, he was in communion with Him, and he possessed spiritual life. This threefold relationship was severed, and Adam became alienated from God, no longer capable of discerning truth. Adam was spiritually dead. In Jesus' words found in John 3:6, "Flesh gives birth to flesh, but the Spirit gives birth to spirit." Adam and Eve bore children after their fallen nature; thus this severed relationship with God was also passed down through each generation. The threefold need of man needed a threefold remedy: reconciliation, illumination, and regeneration. Jesus Christ meets this threefold need as the way, the truth, and the life. George Turner points out that a chronological order is shown here: "The pilgrimage to the city of God requires the one right way, this leads to the truth, which in turn leads to life."[1] How true he is, for we can find truth only when we are on the right path, and it is only in truth that we discover what life really is.

Jesus is the way. Between God and man there was a gulf that was unbridgeable by man. He has certainly attempted to build his own Tower of Babel through his tears, his good works, and even by attending church on a regular basis. Proverbs 14:12 describes the consequences of such attempts: "There is a way that seems right to a man, but in the end it leads to death." Paul, in writing to the Romans, made a similar statement about the condition of all mankind: "All have turned away, they have together become worthless; there is no one that does good, not even one" (3:12). An imperfect man can only develop an imperfect plan. Christ is not merely a guide who can show us the way that man should walk. He is not like Muhammad or Buddha, who sought to reveal the way for their followers. Nor is He merely a teacher who came to enlighten man's understanding about God. He is more than our example, and He is more than a teacher; He *is* the way. He is the way to God, to heaven, and to the forgiveness of sins. He is the way, because

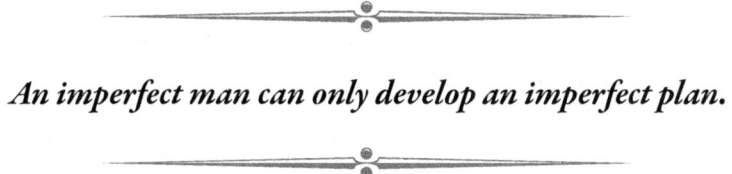

An imperfect man can only develop an imperfect plan.

in His personal advent, the mediation of salvation is given. He is the sole mediator of all men, "for there is one God, and one mediator between God and men, the man Christ Jesus" (1 Tim. 2:5). Jesus as the way can be linked to John 10:9, where He says, "I am the door." He is the only entrance to a relationship with the Father and as such automatically becomes the way for us to live, to conduct business, to treat one another, and to live out our faith. Throughout the history of the church, there have been those who proclaimed to know the way but failed to demonstrate the life of Christ in their daily existence: "If anyone will come after me, he must deny himself and take up his cross and follow me" (Matt. 16:24).

Jesus is the truth. Merrill C. Tenney writes, "Truth is the scarcest commodity in the world. All the philosophers had sought it; none had attained it."[2] To the Greeks, nothing was more desirable than truth, which they equated with knowledge. To the Jews, the very concept of truth rested in God. Today we live in a society that interprets truth in a relative context. What is true for one person may not be true for another. Such a belief distorts a person's view of truth to the extent that they end up like Pilate, who said, "What is truth?" (John 18:38). The irony for Pilate was that Truth was standing right in front of him.

Jesus is the truth, and because of this we can discover the truth about life's values, such as, "A man's life does not consist in the abundance of his possessions" (Luke 12:15). "What good is it for a man to gain the whole world, yet forfeit his soul?" (Mark 8:36). We also discover the truth about ourselves. We learn of our immeasurable worth: "For you created my inmost being; you knit me together in my mother's womb. I praise you because I am fearfully and wonderfully made" (Ps. 139:13–14). We also discover our desperate need for God's grace: "For all have sinned and fall short of the glory of God" (Rom. 3:23), and we learn that in our daily interactions with others, we are held accountable: "Whatever you did for one of the least of these brothers of mine, you did for me" (Matt. 25:40). How we treat one another is the measuring rod by which God judges our love for Him. Turner writes, "Truth is higher and more commanding than creed or orthodoxy. All must ultimately yield to truth."[3]

The only weapon the devil has against us is his lies.

Jesus said, "I am the truth." This self-disclosure was in contrast to what He revealed about the devil, who is a "liar and the father of it" (8:44). The only weapon the devil has against us is his lies. Through these lies he distorts the real picture. Eve saw the fruit and desired it, but it was the devil's lie that first enticed her. I believe behind every temptation there is a lie that distorts the true picture. I remember a woman I once visited who was angry with God because her young child died. She believed God was responsible for his death. It was this lie that kept her from church and the support she desperately needed. It is the truth that exposes the lies.

Jesus is the truth, and as truth, He is the full and final revelation of God. Because He is truth, we can rely upon what He says. When He states,

"No one comes to the Father except through me" (John 14:6), we can be sure that our status, religious beliefs, or position will have no effect on our obtaining a place in heaven. When He says, "Enter through the narrow gate. For wide is the gate and broad is the road that leads to destruction, and many enter through it. But small is the gate and narrow the road that leads to life, and only a few find it," (Matthew 7:13) we had better be determined to be among the "few." Our one question to answer is, "What have I done with Jesus?"

Jesus is the life. Jesus not only gives life, but He is life. The primary interpretation for life here is spiritual life. He told Nicodemus, "Flesh gives birth to flesh, but the Spirit gives birth to spirit" (John 3:6). He shows clearly that spiritual birth can take place only from above. This is part of the meaning in Jesus' statement "I tell you the truth, no one can see the kingdom of God unless he is born again" (3:3). The Greek word translated "again" is *anothen*, from the root word *ano*, which means "from above."⁴ Therefore, the new birth is not only a second birth, referring to the spiritual birth, but it is also a birth that comes from above. The one who *is* life *gives* life.

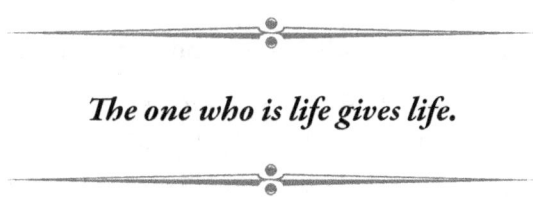

The one who is life gives life.

At the Sermon on the Mount, Jesus portrayed the life He was bringing to man. It is the meek who shall inherit the earth (Matt. 5:5), it is the pure in heart who shall see God (v. 8), it is the merciful who shall obtain mercy (v. 7), and it is the sorrowful who shall be comforted (v. 4). This is in total contrast to the life that is portrayed today by secular society. We hear in commercials and through sitcoms that we must grab all the gusto we can for ourselves because we deserve it. It does not matter who gets in your way; you just walk over them. The life that Jesus laid out for man to live was one that He would live before them, one of self-denial and sacrifice. God's Word is clear that *life* and *existence* are really two different things. First John 5:12 states, "He who has the Son has life; he who does not have the Son of God does not have life."

Life has certain characteristics that can be seen in Christ's relationship with His church. The first is growth. All living things grow and develop. We go from crib, to a tricycle, to a car; we crawl, walk, and then run. Peter says, "Like newborn babies, crave spiritual milk, so that you may grow up in your salvation" (1 Pet. 2:2). Paul chided the Corinthians because he still had to feed them milk instead of meat (1 Cor. 3:2). The natural process of growth would take one from milk to meat. One would never try to feed a steak to an infant, yet at a certain age we expect the child to go from baby food to solid food. The same is true with our spiritual life. Through obedience, the study of God's Word, an active prayer life, and putting our talents to work for Christ, our spirit will grow in wisdom, understanding, and faith.

A second characteristic of life is the ability to perpetuate itself. The command that God gave to Adam and Eve was to "be fruitful and increase in number" (Gen. 1:28). In Jesus' calling of Peter, He said, "Come, follow me . . . and I will make you fishers of men" (Matt. 4:19). Beginning with only twelve men, and one of them a betrayer, the new church had grown to 120 by Pentecost. After Peter's great message on that Pentecost Sunday, the church experienced its first evangelism explosion. Five thousand were saved in a single service. One of the great marks of Christianity has been her missionary endeavor. The church has obeyed the command of her Lord to "go into all the world and preach the good news to all creation"

(Mark 16:15). Jesus said, "I am the life" because He alone is the source of eternal life. Without this life, man becomes prey to spiritual and eternal death. Vincent quotes Thomas à Kempis from his work titled *Imitations of Christ*:

> Without the Way, there is no going; without the Truth, there is no knowing; without the Life, there is no living. I am the Way, which thou oughtest to follow; the Truth which thou oughtest to believe; the Life which thou oughtest to hope for. I am the Way inviolable, the Truth infallible, the Life unending. I am the Way that is straightest, the Truth that is highest, and the Life that is true, the Life blessed, the Life uncreated. If thou remain in My way, though, *thou shalt know the truth*, and the *Truth shall make you free*, and thou shalt lay hold on eternal life. (Italics mine)

Chapter 10

I AM THE TRUE VINE

There is one more of Jesus' images of identification that we need to look at. This probably took place as they were walking toward the garden having left the upper room. As they walked, Jesus drew from another popular image of that day, the vine. Perhaps He even stopped beside one of the vines and held it in His hand as He said, "I am the true vine" (John 15:1). Vineyards were plentiful, and they probably passed several as they made their way through the Judean countryside teaching, preaching, and healing the multitudes. Yet I do not believe Jesus used this image simply because it was in abundance. Like many of the images He used, the vine had a long history in the life of the Jews.

The vine was the Jewish national emblem.[1] On Maccabean coins, Israel was depicted as "the vine of the Lord."[2] Israel as a vine is also seen through the Old Testament. The psalmist wrote, "Return to us, O God Almighty! Look down from heaven and see! Watch over this vine, the root your right hand has planted" (Ps. 80:14–15). Several other passages depict Israel as God's vine as well. Isaiah 5:1–7 describes this relationship and how God took care of Judah as His vine, but it produced "bad fruit" (v. 2). Jeremiah 2:3 portrays Israel as the "first fruits of his harvest." Ezekiel

15:1–8 describes Israel as a vine "not useful for anything" (v. 4), "because they have been unfaithful" (v. 8). One of the chief ornaments made for the temple was "a golden vine with a cluster as large as a man."[3]

In the proper setting, Jesus saying He was the vine could have brought as much of an uprising from the Jews as in John 8:58 when He said, "Before Abraham was born, I am." Israel was considered the vine, and with Jesus' statement, they would have understood Him as saying that He was the true Israel. To them, that would have been as blasphemous as saying He was God. Twice in this section Jesus stated, "I am the vine" (vv. 1, 5), twice He warned against unfruitfulness (vv. 2, 6), and six times He cautioned them to "remain" in Him (vv. 4–10). These three thoughts certainly go together. Jesus is the vine. He is the one who produces the fruit. The branch cannot grow on its own without the vine, let alone bear fruit on its own. It must abide in the vine. The very thought that Jesus cautioned them to abide in the vine makes it very apparent that there are those who abide outside the vine, yet a branch not attached to the vine has no life supply and is therefore dead. Again Paul's words to the Ephesians echo loudly, "You were dead in your transgressions and sins" (Eph. 2:1). Notice Paul says they *were* dead, not that they *are* dead. They had become grafted into the vine (Rom. 11:17), and as a grafted branch, they now received life from the true vine. Life only exists attached to the vine.

Three entities are mentioned here as well: The Father as the gardener, Jesus as the vine, and His followers as the branches. Throughout Jesus' earthly ministry, He pointed to the Father as the one who had sent Him (John 5:43; 8:42). The Father spoke His words of approval at Jesus' baptism and on the Mount of Transfiguration. Both times He said, "This is My Son, whom I love; with him I am well pleased" (Matt. 3:17; 17:5).

Life only exists attached to the vine.

The Father planted the vine: "For God so loved the world, that he gave his one and only Son" (John 3:16), and it was the Father whom Jesus continually glorified. Through Christ's redemptive work, life was made available to all who put their trust in Him: "Yet to all who received him, to those who believed in his name, he gave the right to become children of God" (John 1:12). Speaking to the crowds, Jesus said, "I have come that they may have life, and have it to the full" (John 10:10).

We are the branches. Our life comes from being attached to the vine. No branch can bear fruit of itself, and no man can be fruitful unless he remains attached to Christ, the Vine (v. 4). What futility in trying to produce fruit on our own! This was the case with Israel. Jeremiah was given a message from God to deliver to them: "I had planted you like a choice vine of sound and reliable stock. How then did you turn against me into a corrupt, wild vine?" (Jer. 2:21). Without the life-flowing sap from vine to branch, the branch becomes unfruitful. Fruit is a sign of life, not the cause of life.

Many people are depending on their good works to get them to heaven but will be greatly disappointed when they discover that they are nothing more than a fruitless branch. It is life in Christ that produces good works, not vice versa. Jesus makes it clear that apart from Him, we can do nothing (John 15:5). It is the fruit that is evidence of life in the vine. This is what James was talking about when he said he would show his faith by his works. He did not mean works saved him, but the works were the fruit of his life in Christ.

There are times when the leaves of a vine are full and green and give the appearance of a fruitful vine, yet they produce no fruit. This was the case in Mark 11:13 (also found in Matthew 21:19). Jesus saw a fig tree in leaf and went up to it to get some figs, but it had none. Even though abundant in leaves, it was fruitless. Jesus then pronounced a curse on the tree that it would never again bear fruit. There are those within the church who display an abundance of leaves (good works), yet these leaves cover the fact that their lives are unfruitful. Anyone can accomplish good works, but it takes a connection to the Vine (living through the power of Christ) to produce fruit.

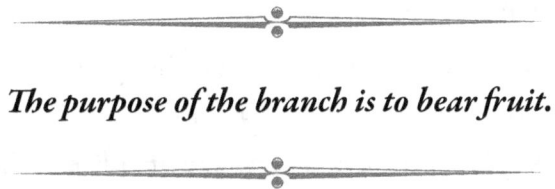

The purpose of the branch is to bear fruit.

We are told that the branches that do not bear fruit are cut off. How can a branch attached to the vine not bear fruit? Perhaps Judas is a good example. Had not this man walked with Jesus and witnessed the miracles as others did? Had he not listened with the others to the message from Jesus' lips and observed the love wherewith He touched people's lives? Yet he was fruitless. While in the presence of the Vine, he did not take in the nourishment needed to live, namely faith. Unconfessed sin will block the flow of life to the branch, as well as selfishness, bitterness, and an unforgiving spirit. The purpose of the branch is to bear fruit. During His Sermon on the Mount, Jesus instructed the people to "let your light shine before men, that they may see your good deeds [fruit] and praise your Father in heaven" (Matt. 5:16).

When a branch does bear fruit, the Father prunes it so it will be even more fruitful (John 15:2). I remember a farmer who was attempting to raise a prize-winning pumpkin. He provided it with rich soil, plenty of space to grow, sufficient water—everything it needed was supplied. When a good-sized pumpkin started growing on a vine, he began to prune off the leaves and other runners so that all the nutrients went to that pumpkin, making it even larger. At the end of the season, he had a 265-pound pumpkin. It was indeed a prizewinner, taking second place in the local competition.

There are things that are a part of our lives that drain the strength from us that is necessary to bear good fruit. It may be bad habits, a quick tongue, lack of discipline, or a number of other things that keep us from bearing the fruit that God wants us to bear. The apostle Paul tells us what allowed him to bear fruit for God: "I have been crucified with Christ and I no longer live, but Christ lives in me. The life I live in the body, I live by faith in the Son of God, who loved me, and gave himself for me" (Gal. 2:20). It is this life given by the Vine that enabled Paul to also say, "I can do everything through him who gives me strength" (Phil. 4:13). Jesus is the true Vine, giving life to all who are attached to Him. The symbolism used is governed by the opening words, "I AM." Jesus is all that the vine symbolizes.

CONCLUSION

We have seen how Jesus emphatically proclaimed His divinity. Drawing from a variety of common images, He redefined them and drew them into His personhood. Jesus took these different opportunities to reveal His true nature by offering living water to a Samaritan woman. He calmed the fears of men through the peace His presence brought in the midst of a stormy sea. The people asked for a sign like unto manna, and He boldly proclaimed to be the only true bread that could satisfy man's hunger, bread that came down from heaven. In a territory where sheep were a common sight, Jesus gave new insight into the true sheep of God and the true Shepherd. When Martha affirmed her belief in the resurrection, Jesus led her from a religious concept to the living Resurrection. When Thomas was concerned that he would not know the way, Jesus assured him that the Way knew him. Drawing their attention to the vine and the branches and how important it is for the branch to stay connected to the vine, Jesus proclaimed to be the true Vine and the source of their fruitfulness. From this collection of sayings, there is only one conclusion to draw about the identity of Jesus Christ. From the Old Testament through the New, Jesus Christ is seen as the eternal I AM and man's only hope of redemption.

One of the great truths that comes from this study is that Jesus can be known only by spiritual insight. Over and over He urged the multitudes to let His works speak for themselves, but they refused. The Pharisees and chief priests pondered for many hours the manner and time of the Messiah's coming, but they could not see Him when He appeared. Today is no different. Since September 11, 2001, many have turned back to religion, but it is a religion devoid of truth because it lacks the Truth. It is a religion that lacks life because the one who is Life has been left out. Jesus' words to the church of Laodicea speak loudly to the world today: "Here I am! I stand at the door and knock. If anyone hears my voice and opens the door, I will come in and eat with him, and he with me" (Rev. 3:20).

There will always be those who question the validity of Jesus' claims. They will see Jesus as a great teacher or even a prophet, but not as the eternal Son of God, not as the means of salvation. Their view will not be based on any philosophical choice, but on a moral one. It is much easier to ignore the words of a man than to ignore the words of God. To accept Jesus' claims as the eternal God is to make one accountable to follow what He says. Their deception, however, is that whether they accept Jesus' claims or not, they are accountable. Jesus says to the world today, "I AM," and in saying that, He says everything!

A Personal Note

Have you made that step of making Jesus Christ Lord of your life? You may have been raised in the church, and you may even believe that Jesus is the Son of God. You may believe that He was born of a virgin, walked among men, died on a cross, and was raised the third day, but have you asked Him to be your personal Savior? If not, I have included a simple prayer that puts what you believe into action:

Lord Jesus, I believe that You are God's Son and that You died for my sins. I believe that You were raised to life and sit at the right hand of God the Father, and that one day You are coming again. Lord, I am not sure I will be ready, so right here, right now, I confess and turn from my sins and ask You to forgive me. I invite You to come live in my heart, and by Your grace, I will follow You. Thank You, Jesus, for saving me!

There are only three questions I need to ask:
1. Was your prayer sincere?
2. If so, where are your sins?
3. Where is Jesus right now?

I encourage you to pray and read your Bible (I suggest the gospel of John), and seek out other Christians who can help you live out your faith. God bless you, and know that God loves you!

ABOUT THE AUTHOR

Terry Morris is a licensed professional counselor with a history in Bible, and counseling. He graduated from Ohio Christian University, formerly Circleville Bible College, with a BA in Bible. He attended Wesley Biblical Seminary, completing his master's in theology at Christian Bible College. He earned a second master's degree from the University of West Alabama in Counseling/Psychology. He served as youth pastor, associate pastor, and senior pastor before pursuing a ministry among children and adolescents with emotional and behavioral problems. Mr. Morris has worked alongside the Georgia Department of Child and Family Services, providing in-home counseling services for families who have been involved with the state. Mr. Morris is currently on staff at Wellsprings Psychological Resources in Franklin Springs, Georgia, and is also involved with the Ark Family Preservation Center, a nonprofit organization that is dedicated to strengthening and preserving families through parenting education. Mr. Morris is also a nationally certified anger-management specialist and provides anger-management classes through the Ark.

Endnotes

Introduction

[1] H. Orton Wiley, *Christian Theology: Vol. 2* (Kansas City, Mo.: Beacon Hill Press, 1952), p. 157.

[2] Ibid.

[3] Ibid., p. 158.

[4] Ibid., p. 165.

Chapter 1

[1] Alexander Maclaren, *Expositions of the Holy Scripture: Exodus, Leviticus, and Numbers* (Cincinnati, Oh.: Jennings and Graham, n.d.), p. 20.

[2] Ibid.

[3] Josh McDowell and Bart Larson, *Jesus: A Biblical Defense of His Deity* (San Bernadino, Calif.: Here's Life Publishers, Inc., 1983), p. 22.

[4] Alexander Maclaren, op. cit.; p. 23.

[5] Lee Haines, editor, *The Wesleyan Bible Commentary, Vol. 1* (Grand Rapids, Mich.: William B. Eerdmans Sons, 1967), p. 180.

Chapter 2

[1] George and Julius Mantley, *The Gospel According to John* (Grand Rapids, Mich.: William B. Eerdmans Publishing Company, n.d.), p. 167.

[2] Ibid.

[3] Philip Harner, *The "I AM" of the Fourth Gospel* (Philadelphia, Pa.: The Fortress Press, 1970), p. 3.

[4] Ibid.

[5] Ibid.

[6] C. H. Dodd, *The Interpretation of the Fourth Gospel* (Cambridge: University Press, 1953), p. 93.

[7] Philip Harner, op. cit., p. 3.

[8] H. E. Dana and Julius Mantley, *A Manual Grammar of the Greek New Testament* (Toronto: The Macmillan Company, 1955), p. 137.

[9] Roger L. Fredrikson, *The Communicator's Commentary: Vol. 4, John* (Waco, Tex.: Word Books, 1985), p. 101.

[10] Leon Morris, *Reflections on the Gospel of John, Vol. 2* (Grand Rapids, Mich.: Baker Book House, 1987), p. 215.

[11] W. J. Hickie, *Greek-English Lexicon to the New Testament* (Grand Rapids, Mich.: Baker Book House, 1977), p. 31.

[12] Leon Morris, op. cit., p. 216.

[13] Roger Fredrikson, op. cit., p. 127.

[14] Ibid., p. 262.

[15] A. Plummer, *The Gospel According to St. John* (Cambridge: University Press, 1882), p. 308.

[16] F. F. Bruce, *The Gospel of John* (Grand Rapids, Mich.: William B. Eerdmans Publishing Company, 1983), p. 341.

Chapter 3

[1] Roger Fredrikson, op. cit., p. 158.

[2] Leon Morris, op. cit., p. 313.

[3] Roger Fredrikson, op. cit., p. 159.

[4] Arthur W. Pink, *Expositions of the Gospel of John* (Grand Rapids, Mich.: Zondervan Publishing House, 1980), p. 56.

[5] Donald Macleod, *The Person of Christ* (Downers Grove, Ill.: InterVarsity Press, 1998), p. 46.

[6] Leon Morris, op. cit., p. 344.

Chapter 4

[1] Fulton J. Sheen, *Life of Christ* (New York: McGraw-Hill Book Company, Inc., 1958), p. 150.

[2] Ibid.

[3] Leon Morris, op. cit., p. 229.

[4] Fulton Sheen, op. cit., p. 154.

Chapter 5

[1] Craig Koester, *Symbolism in the Fourth Gospel* (Minneapolis, Minn.: Fortress Press, 1995), p. 128.

[2] Ibid.

[3] Marvin Vincent, *Word Studies of the New Testament, Vol. 2* (New York: Charles Scribner's Sons, 1967), p. 167.

[4] Craig Koestner, op. cit., p. 141.

[5] Marvin Vincent, op. cit., p. 167.

[6] George Stewart, *Jesus Said, "I AM"* (New York: Harper Brothers Publishers, 1934), p. 49.

Chapter 6

[1] Roger Fredrikson, op. cit., p. 179.
[2] Leon Morris, op. cit., p. 377.
[3] C. K. Barrett, op. cit., p. 308.
[4] George Turner, op. cit., p. 215.
[5] Arthur Pink, op. cit., p. 113.
[6] Phillip Keller, *A Shepherd Looks at the Good Shepherd and His Sheep* (Grand Rapids, Mich.: Zondervan Publishing House, 1978), p. 87.

Chapter 7

[1] Phillip Keller, op. cit., p. 109.
[2] Bob Boyd, *The Testimony of a Sheep* (Scranton, Penn.: Robert T. Boyd, 1962), p. 8.
[3] Arthur Pink, op. cit., p. 125.
[4] Ibid., p. 187.

Chapter 8

[1] Arthur Pink, op. cit., p. 187.
[2] John Exell, *The Biblical Illustrator: St. John, Vol. 1* (Grand Rapids, Mich.: Baker Book House, 1953), p. 269.
[3] C. H. Dodd, op. cit., p. 365.

Chapter 9

[1] George Turner, op. cit., p. 288.
[2] Merrill C. Tenney, *John: The Gospel of Belief* (Grand Rapids, Mich.: William B. Eerdmans Publishing Company, 1948), p. 288.
[3] George Turner, op. cit., p. 285.
[4] W.J. Hickie, op. cit., p. 17.
[5] Marvin Vincent, op. cit., p. 216.

Chapter 10

[1] Merrill C. Tenney, op. cit., p. 216.

[2] George Turner, op. cit., p. 295.

[3] Fredrikson, op. cit., p. 235.

Bibliography

Barrett, C. K. *The Gospel According to St. John*. London, England: S.P.C.K. 1955.

Bruce, F. F. *The Gospel of John*. Grand Rapids, Michigan: William B. Eerdmans Publishing Company. 1983.

Dodd, C. H. *The Interpretation of the Fourth Gospel*. Cambridge, England: University Press. 1953.

Exell, John. *The Biblical Illustrator: St. John, Vol. II*. Grand Rapids, Michigan: Baker Book House. 1953.

Fredrikson, Roger. *The Communicator's Commentary: Vol. 4, John*. Waco, Texas: Word Books. 1985.

Haines, Lee. ed. *The Wesleyan Bible Commentary, Vol. 1*. Grand Rapids, Michigan: William B. Eerdmans Sons. 1967.

Halley, Henry. *Halley's Bible Handbook*. Grand Rapids, Michigan: Zondervan Publishing House. 1959.

Harner, Phillip. *The "I AM" of the Fourth Gospel*. Philadelphia, Pennsylvania: The Fortress Press. 1970.

Hickie, W. J. *Greek-English Lexicon to the New Testament*. Grand Rapids, Michigan: Baker Cook House. 1977.

Keller, Phillip. *A Shepherd Looks at the Good Shepherd and His Sheep*. Grand Rapids, Michigan: Zondervan Publishing House. 1978.

Koestner, Craig. *Symbolism in the Fourth Gospel*. Minneapolis, Minnesota: The Fortress Press. 1995.

Maclaren, Alexander. *Expositions of the Holy Scripture: Exodus, Leviticus, and Numbers*. Cincinnati, Ohio: Jennings and Graham. N.D.

Macleod, Donald. *The Person of Christ*. Downers Grove, Illinois: InterVarsity Press. 1998.

McDowell, Josh and Bart Larson. *Jesus: A Biblical Defense of His Deity*. San Bernardino, California: Here's Life Publishers, Inc. 1983.

Morris, Leon. *Reflections on the Gospel of John, Vol. II*. Grand Rapids, Michigan: Baker Book House. 1987.

Pink, Arthur. *Exposition of the Gospel of John*. Grand Rapids, Michigan: Zondervan Publishing House. 1945.

Plummer, A. *The Gospel According to St. John*. Cambridge, United Kingdom: University Press. 1882.

Sheen, Fulton J. *Life of Christ*. New York, New York: McGraw-Hill Book Company, Inc. 1958.

Stewart, George. *Jesus Said, "I AM."* New York, New York: Harpers Brothers Publishers. 1934.

Tenney, Merrill C. *John: The Gospel of Belief*. Grand Rapids, Michigan: William B. Eerdmans Publishing Company. 1948.

Turner, George Allen and Julius Mantley. *The Gospel According to John*. Grand Rapids, Michigan: William B. Eerdmans Publishing Company. N.D.

Vincent, Marvin. *Word Studies of the New Testament*. New York, New York: Charles Scribner's Sons. 1967.

Wiley, H. Orton. *Christian Theology: Vol. II*. Kansas City, Missouri: Beacon Hill Press. 1952.

www.ingramcontent.com/pod-product-compliance
Lightning Source LLC
LaVergne TN
LVHW051955060526
838201LV00059B/3662